STUDY GUIDE
to accompany

SOCIOLOGY

FROM CONCEPTS
TO PRACTICE

*

STUDY GUIDE
to accompany

S O C I O L O G Y

FROM CONCEPTS TO PRACTICE

BERNARD PHILLIPS
Boston University

Fitz Memorial Library

Endicott College
Beverly, Massachusetts 01915

McGraw-Hill Book Company
New York   St. Louis   San Francisco   Auckland   Bogotá   Düsseldorf
Johannesburg   London   Madrid   Mexico   Montreal   New Delhi   Panama
Paris   São Paulo   Singapore   Sydney   Tokyo   Toronto

Study Guide to accompany SOCIOLOGY:
From Concepts to Practice

Copyright © 1979 by McGraw-Hill, Inc. All rights reserved.
Printed in the United States of America. No part of this publication
may be reproduced, stored in a retrieval system, or transmitted, in any
form or by any means electronic, mechanical, photocopying, recording, or
otherwise, without the prior written permission of the publisher.

ISBN 0-07-049793-1

HM
51
P48   47511
V12

1 2 3 4 5 6 7 8 9 0   WHWH   7 8 3 2 1 0 9

PREFACE TO THE STUDENT

This Study Guide is designed to help students using Sociology: From Concepts to Practice to achieve mastery over the materials contained in that text. It cannot substitute for the text, but it may aid you in organizing your studies so that you will be able to clearly demonstrate your knowledge of sociology.

The overall objective of the text and Study Guide is to help you to learn and apply a new language: the language of sociology. Many of its terms--such as "role," "crime," "institution," and "community"--appear to be quite familiar. Yet the sociological definitions of these terms depart somewhat from everyday usages and, by so doing, provide new dimensions of understanding. Many other sociological terms--such as "structural-functionalism," "relative deprivation," "paradigm," and "resocialization"--are new to most students. And still other terms--such as "social class," "ethnic group," "deviant behavior," and "legitimation"--fall somewhere in between terms which are quite familiar and quite unfamiliar.

This vocabulary of sociology can help us all to locate and deal with forces within society that operate on us, such as the pressures to conform to widely accepted ways of thinking and doing. Our familiar world of everyday life, which we tend to take for granted, is only partially understood by us. And the language of sociology can help us to penetrate its unknowns. Further, such knowledge can place us in a far better position to deal with everyday personal problems as well as large-scale societal problems.

The language of sociology is, then, the key to learning sociology. And, just as in the case of any foreign language, your learning is helped the more you can become actively involved with it. For example, the passive reading of a passage in Spanish or French does not go very far in helping you to understand or speak those languages. Neither will a passive reading of the text help you very much with mastery over the language of sociology. A good deal more is required, yet none of the work is difficult. Rather, it is a matter of proceeding in a directed or organized fashion so as to gradually build up one's knowledge. There are a great many different ways to proceed, and you should feel free to invent the one most suited to your own preferences. The following listing of procedures may, however, prove to be helpful:

READING (Text)

1. Objectives: A list of objectives appear at the beginning of each chapter in the text. Read these to gain a
general understanding of the directions taken in the
chapter. Also, try to understand their importance for
you in more personal terms.

2. Reading with objectives in mind: As you proceed
with the reading of any portion of the text, try to keep
in mind the objective for that portion. By so doing,
your reading will be more active and you will tend to
retain more information. Of course, feel free to modify,
eliminate, or supplement the listed objectives, depending on your own interests and those of your instructor.
But in any case, it is important to have some objectives.

3. Key terms: Each term within the sociological language
appears in italics in the text and is defined in italics
on its first appearance. It is then generally followed
by an example or by being used to clarify something.
Pay special attention to these terms and illustrations.
Make sure you understand what each term means.

4. Summary: At the close of each chapter a summary
appears. Even if you believe that you understand the
chapter, a reading of the summary can be very helpful.
For example, many of the sociological terms are used
in the summary. Also, the summary can help you to develop a feeling or perspective for the chapter as a unit.

5. Glossary: All of the sociological terms defined
within the text are repeated--in the order in which they
appeared--in the glossary after the summary at the end
of each chapter. Although you may already have a passive knowledge of the meaning of each term, here is an
opportunity to make your knowledge more active. For
example, you might wish to cover the terms to see if
you can recall them from their definitions.

REVIEW (Study Guide)

6. Overview: Within the Study Guide, the material for
each chapter begins with a one-paragraph overview con-
taining the chapter's highlights. Once again, even
though you believe you already know what is in the chapter, a careful reading of the overview will help you
cement your knowledge together.

7. Synopsis: Here is a summary of the chapter--immediately following the overview--that is twice as detailed as the one appearing in the text. All of the sociological terms are used here. And, again, continuing to read material where these terms are used helps to make them more meaningful, just as in the case of a foreign language.

8. Self-Quiz: Multiple Choice: A total of twenty multiple-choice questions is the largest section of the self-quiz for each chapter. They are designed to cover important material from all parts of the chapter. Treat this as an actual examination: Do not look up the answers until after you have answered all of the questions. Otherwise, the questions will not result in as much active learning on your part.

9. Self-Quiz: Concept Recognition: The definitions for the chapter concepts are presented here in random order. Once again, treat this as a genuine examination, filling in the blanks with the correct terms. These terms are the keys to learning how to use the language of sociology.

10. Self-Quiz: True-False: Treat these as a supplement to the multiple-choice questions; they cover additional material in the chapter. Once again, do not look up the correct answers until you have recorded your own answers.

11. Self-Quiz: Concept Definition: All of the terms defined in a given chapter are presented here in random order. Proceed to define them in your own words: in this way, they can more easily become an active part of your vocabulary.

FURTHER STUDY

12. Additional Reading in the Text: The self-quiz can point up weaknesses in your knowledge of a given chapter. Go back to the chapter and focus on those parts or concepts you have done poorly on.

13. Other Additional Reading: At the end of each text chapter is a list of four books, with each described in a sentence or two. If you can make time to read an occasional extra book, you can learn to make sociology one of the strong points in your academic knowledge.

14. Essays in Response to Objectives: Each of the objectives at the beginning of a text chapter is stated as a question. Proceed to answer these questions in essay form, devoting about a page to each question. If necessary, review the material in the chapter that bears on a given question prior to answering it.

15. Using Concepts from Previous Chapters: Add an additional page to each essay by applying concepts defined in previous chapters to your discussion. Look over the lists of concepts in the "Concept Definition" parts of the Study Guide to get ideas as to which terms might be used.

And beyond understanding the language of sociology lies an ability to use such understanding in everyday life. In my own view, no individual has--as yet--proceeded very far in this direction. The student who wishes to follow this path need not obtain advanced degrees in sociology, although a lifetime of effort is required. As for the rewards of using sociology in our daily routine, they cannot be estimated since we are on uncertain ground. In that direction lies the promise of sociology, a promise which has as yet been only partly fulfilled.

CONTENTS

Sociology:The Science of Society

1

OVERVIEW

Sociology emerged in Europe in the middle of the
19th century, a time when the industrial revolution was
gathering momentum and overturning traditional patterns
of social life. Then as now, sociology helps people to
question taken-for-granted assumptions about life in
society. For example, the idea that powerful pressures
to conform to group behavior operate on the individual
is set in opposition to the widespread assumption that
the individual is relatively free to do as he or she
pleases. Along with such ideas, sociology emphasizes
the use of scientific research procedures, as illustrated
by Durkheim's classic study of suicide in Europe.

SYNOPSIS

1.1 Sociology Defined

  a Questioning Taken-For-Granted Assumptions

Flatland, a classic science fiction story, tells of
a world of two-dimensional creatures who reject the
possibility that a three-dimensional world exists.
How willing are we to question our own fundamental
assumptions? Are we very much like the Flatlanders
in this respect? For example, do we assume that
aggression is part of human nature and do we refuse

1

to consider evidence to the contrary? The study of
sociology can help us to question such assumptions
that many of us normally take for granted or view
as simply common sense, providing us with information collected by sociologists to compare with existing beliefs about society. But sociology can be
of little help if we are unwilling to open up to
the possibility that our existing assumptions are
incorrect or inadequate.

b Origins of Sociology

Auguste Comte (1798-1857) coined the term "sociology" (the science of society). Along with 18th-
century Enlightenment thinkers like Voltaire, he
dreamed of a society based on reason. He was im-
pressed by the successes of the physical sciences
and believed that the scientific method could also
be applied to explain events in society. Such explanations were in great demand, as Europe was
experiencing severe social problems as a result of
the rapid changes associated with the industrial
revolution.

1.2 Images of Sociology

a The Physicist

Sociology has a great deal in common with many
other disciplines, such as physics. Einstein was
the physical world as a huge puzzle waiting to be
solved. Similarly, sociologists see society as
presenting us with unknowns about the nature of
human behavior. They attempt to develop awareness
of the forces involved (sociological consciousness),
an awareness that--if attained by people in society--
might help them deal with their problems. In addition to being located in academic institutions,
sociologists do research in governmental and private agencies as well as work in applied capacities
such as market research.

b The Dramatist

Henrik Ibsen's A Doll's House reveals his ability
to be deeply critical of the situation in which
married women found themselves in the late 19th
century. His character, Nora, rebels against a
life in which she is treated as no more than a doll
by her husband. Ibsen's ability to envision a

society very different from that of his own--where
women would be treated as full human beings--illus-
trates the sociological imagination (ability to
image alternatives to existing societal patterns).
Sociologists--more than dramatists--emphasize the
repeated application of special concepts to a
variety of situations.

c The Detective

Sherlock Holmes not only uncovers facts but also
deduces the relationships among them. In The Rei-
gate Puzzle, for example, he is able to analyze a
scrap of paper with a few words on it and draw 26
deductions about the individuals who wrote them.
The detective, as distinct from the physicist or
the sociologist, is primarily concerned with using
available knowledge to help solve problems in society (the enforcement of the law). Yet although
sociology does not emphasize the application of
knowledge (and, instead, stresses the accumulation
of fundamental knowledge), there is increasing
attention being paid to sociological practice
(applying sociological knowledge to human problems).

1.3 Social Structure and Social Change

a Social Interaction and Social Relationships

Whereas social interaction may be illustrated by a
one-time situation in which two or more people
affect one another, a social relationship is a continuing pattern of such interaction. It is sociology's broad concern with interactions and relationships of all kinds that distinguish it from
disciplines like economics and political science,
which focus on only certain kinds of interactions
and relationships. Social relationships can be
highly influential on those involved in them.

b Social Structure

People are tied together in other ways than through
social relationships. The concept of social structure (shared beliefs, interests and social relationships) is more comprehensive. In a small group as
well as in society as a whole a web of social structure is formed. For example, people who interact
learn about beliefs and interests that they share
and--with continuing interaction--tend to develop
additional shared beliefs and interests.

3

c   Social Change

Social structures are continually changing. This
phenomenon of social change--or alteration of social
structure in a given direction--is illustrated by
the shift from a preindustrial or agricultural
society to an industrial society. Accompanying this
economic shift are many profound alterations in
society. For example, Tonnies has discussed a
change from the gemeinschaft (a social structure
emphasizing close personal relationships) to the
gesellschaft (a social structure stressing impersonality and social isolation). Some other sociologists, such as Durkheim, have seen the changed
social relationships in a more positive light.

1.4   Scientific Method

a   An Illustration: Durkheim's Suicide

Although Durkheim felt that an industrial society
tended to produce a new kind of social solidarity,
in contrast to Tonnies' emphasis on impersonality,
he became interested in investigating the impact
of the absence of social relationships or social
solidarity on the individual. In his classic study
of suicide, for example, he found that husbands
with children are far less likely to commit suicide
than husbands without children. And husbands without children are less likely to commit suicide than
widowers without children.

b   Research as a Continuing Process

Durkheim's study illustrates the four stages of the
scientific method: (1) defining a problem, (2) developing hypotheses for solving the problem, (3)
testing the hypotheses, and (4) analyzing the results as well as drawing conclusions. But the
research process does not end with that fourth stage,
for the scientific method incorporates the assumption that knowledge is infinite. Each study only
goes a certain distance, and its conclusions then
become the basis for a new definition of the problem. For example, Durkheim tended to take for
granted the accuracy of the official statistics he
used, yet contemporary investigators of suicide
suggest some of the complex factors which produce
such statistics. If suicide as a cause of death

is viewed negatively in society, then family and friends will tend to put pressure on officials to categorize the cause of death differently.

1.5 Plan of This Book

Parts One, Two, and Three introduce the reader to social structure, personality structure, and theory and methods, respectively. The major portion of the book is then given over to a detailed examination of social structure from three different perspectives in parts Four, Five and Six. These perspectives correspond to the three aspects of the definition of social structure: (1) shared beliefs (stratification), (2) shared interests (institutions), and (3) social relationships (groups). Part Seven, Biological and Physical Structures, introduces structures in addition to social and personality structures. And, finally, in Part Eight we take up systematically a topic pursued throughout this volume: social change.

SELF-QUIZ

Multiple Choice: In the space provided, enter the letter of the answer that best completes the question.

_____ 1. Sociologists are like the square in <u>Flatland</u> in that

  a) they question basic assumptions people take for granted
  b) they see people relating to one another primarily as equals
  c) they believe that groups are more powerful than individuals
  d) they are searching for the fourth dimension of space-time

_____ 2. The term "sociology" means, literally,

  a) research on the human being
  b) the study of human institutions
  c) the science of society
  d) collecting information on the community

_____ 3. Sociological consciousness is best illustrated by

  a) the detective who solves problems
  b) the dramatist who imagines a different kind of society
  c) the psychologist who administers tests to people
  d) the individual who is aware of people's attitudes towards her

_____ 4. For Goffman, who uses the language of the theatre, "front" is

  a) the region of the stage closest to the footlights
  b) behavior which is obviously out of character
  c) the part of a performance which defines the situation for the audience
  d) the stance taken so as not to "give the show away"

_____ 5. An activity of the detective best illustrating sociological practice is

  a) learning what causes criminal behavior

b) using knowledge of criminal behavior to solve a case
c) developing a personal commitment to eliminate crime
d) making deductions about the relationships among facts

6. Social interaction is best illustrated by

a) two strangers in an elevator who chance to look at one another at the same time
b) the relationship between a radio performer and her audience
c) slipping and falling on a tangerine peel
d) shared beliefs, interests and social relationships

7. Social structure

a) can be developed in an instant, such as love at first sight
b) is one kind of group
c) is illustrated by hierarchies and groups
d) does not change

8. If Tonnies' view of social change were correct, then

a) life is getting better and better with the growth of cities
b) people are losing their close relationships as industrialization continues
c) both closer relationships and more superficial relationships are becoming prevalent in large cities
d) people are becoming less and less separated from one another

9. If Weber's view of social change were correct, then

a) the revolt against bureaucracy will continually increase
b) an interest in mythology and religion will become more important
c) organizations will become ever more complex
d) people will relate to one another as equals to an increasing degree

10. If Durkheim's study of suicide applies to contemporary American society, then

    a) men who marry and have children will have a great tendency to commit suicide
    b) widowers with children will have less tendency to commit suicide than widowers without children
    c) men who marry and have no children will have a greater tendency to suicide than widowers with children
    d) widowers will have less suicidal tendencies than men whose wives are still alive

11. A society like <u>Flatland</u>

    a) would tend to change rapidly
    b) would tend to value freedom of speech
    c) would tend to value equality
    d) would tend to change slowly

12. Sociology is best illustrated by

    a) gathering information on the material wealth of a nation
    b) taking appropriate action to eliminate a slum
    c) studying changes in the basic goals people have in society
    d) calculating the levels of pollution in a city at different times

13. To develop a sociological consciousness, it is most important to

    a) become committed to solving societal problems
    b) actively try to solve problems in the community
    c) try to "put sociology to work" in everyday situations
    d) increase your awareness of the social relationships involved in your everyday life

14. For a lecturer, one "region"--using Goffman's term from the language of the theatre, is

    a) the front of the lecture room
    b) the small area, not visible to the audience behind the podium

c) the blackboard
d) the proscenium

_____ 15. One difference between the sociologist and
the detective is that

   a) the sociologist emphasizes the accumulation
      of a body of knowledge
   b) the detective does not examine the relation-
      ships among facts
   c) the sociologist does not attempt to solve
      problems
   d) the detective does not attempt to unearth
      knowledge

_____ 16. Social structure, social relationship and
social interaction are related in that

   a) social structure includes social relation-
      ships
   b) social relationships include social struc-
      ture of all kinds
   c) social interactions includes social rela-
      tionships
   d) social interaction includes social struc-
      ture

_____ 17. Social structure

   a) is fixed, just as physical structure is
      fixed
   b) is a system of shared beliefs
   c) includes both large and small groups
   d) is limited to groups as large as societies

_____ 18. Social change

   a) is any kind of change in society
   b) is any kind of change in a small group
   c) is a change in one particular direction for
      any size group
   d) is a change in one particular direction of
      social structure

_____ 19. The scientific method

   a) involves defining a problem, constructing
      hypotheses, testing hypotheses, and analysis
      and conclusions
   b) is a tentative idea about how to solve a

            problem
        c) is a technique which arrives at final truth
        d) is a system of tentative ideas about how to
            solve a problem

____ 20. Durkheim's study of suicide

        a) concluded that social interaction causes
            suicide
        b) includes the conclusion that the absence of
            social relationships is associated with a
            tendency to commit suicide
        c) includes the conclusion that suicides tend
            to strengthen social relationships
        d) includes the conclusion that social inter-
            action, suicide rates and social relation-
            ships are parts of social structure

Concept Recognition: Write the concept or term in the
blank space next to its definition.

_____ 1. Action that mutually affects two
or more individuals.

_____ 2. A tentative idea or statement
about how to solve a problem or about the nature of
reality.

_____ 3. The science of society.

_____ 4. The application of sociological
knowledge to human problems.

_____ 5. A process for developing knowledge based on (1) defining a problem, (2) constructing hypotheses or ideas about how to solve the problem, (3) testing these hypotheses, and (4) analyzing
the results and drawing conclusions.

_____ 6. A society in which a substantial
proportion of the labor force is involved in the
production of goods.

_____ 7. A continuing pattern of social
interaction.

_____ 8. Alteration of social structure
in a given direction.

_____ 9. A social structure emphasizing

close personal relationships.

_____ 10. Awareness of the forces at work
in society.

True/False: Enter "T" for true or "F" for false for the best answer to the statement.

_____ 1. Sociology arose at approximately the same time as the emergence of rapid changes in society associated with the industrial revolution.

_____ 2. Sociologists generally are far more interested in applying existing knowledge to solve societal problems than in searching for new knowledge.

_____ 3. Sociologists do not tend to repeat themselves by using the same terms over and over again to gain insight into situations in society.

_____ 4. It is essential to become a professional sociologist in order to learn how to use the sociological imagination.

_____ 5. Common-sense knowledge about society is frequently incorrect or misleading.

_____ 6. Social relationships tend to be more influential on those involved than social interaction outside of such relationships.

_____ 7. Sociologists in American society form a social structure.

_____ 8. Tonnies would say that our society today is primarily a Gemeinschaft.

_____ 9. Lester Frank Ward saw industrial societies as progressing toward the reduction of planning.

_____ 10. Durkheim put forward the hypothesis that the absence of social relationships tends to be associated with a tendency to commit suicide.

Concept definition: Write the definition of the concept or term appearing on the left in the blank space next to it.

1. theory _____

_____

2. preindustrial society _____

_____

3. social structure _____

_____

4. sociological imagination _____

_____

5. gesellschaft _____

_____

6. social change _____

_____

7. social relationship _____

_____

8. scientific method _____

_____

9. sociology _____

_____

10. social interaction _____

_____

ANSWERS

Self Quiz

1.	a	6.	a	11.	d	16.	a
2.	c	7.	c	12.	c	17.	c
3.	d	8.	b	13.	d	18.	d
4.	c	9.	c	14.	b	19.	a
5.	b	10.	b	15.	a	20.	b

Concept Recognition

1.	social interaction	6.	industrial society
2.	hypothesis	7.	social relationship
3.	sociology	8.	social change
4.	sociological practice	9.	gemeinschaft
5.	scientific method	10.	sociological consciousness

True-False

1.	T	6.	T
2.	F	7.	T
3.	F	8.	F
4.	F	9.	F
5.	T	10.	T

Concept Definition

See Glossary in back of this booklet

Culture
2

OVERVIEW

Language is the basis for culture, which provides
people with a blueprint for life in society. This blueprint includes norms and values, or widely shared expectations and goals. The latter are illustrated in American society by achievement and success, activity and
work, material comfort, equality, freedom and democracy.
The power of culture is illustrated by ethnocentrism, or
fundamental perspectives rooted in one's own culture
which tend to downgrade perspectives from other cultures.
Cultural change is illustrated by the movement toward
equality of the sexes, and sub-cultural change by community development in Huasahuasi, Peru.

SYNOPSIS

2.1 The Biological Basis for Culture

An understanding of culture in human societies must
begin with some understanding of human biology,
which affects all aspects of our behavior. Over
some four billion years the process of biological
evolution has resulted in a continuing alteration
of life forms. Homo sapiens, in addition to having
acute vision, a long life span, the ability to walk
erect and an opposable thumb, possesses a number of
attributes associated with the development of a com-

14

plex language and speech: the ability to emit a
variety of sounds, a large brain, and a long period
of dependence on the part of the infant. Linguistic
capability gives to Homo sapiens the capacity to
achieve fundamental changes in behavior without
waiting for the very long process of biological
adaptation. We can evolve in other than biological
ways.

2.2   Language and Culture

a   The Nature and Functions of Language

Language is a system of symbols enabling us to communicate (especially through speech and writing)
with others and with ourselves through inner speech
or thought. Thus, it helps us enormously to adapt,
bringing to our every situation the fruits of other
experiences. It is not merely a passive instrument.
For example, the three words for snow in Eskimo
alerts the individual to look for different kinds
of snow.

b   Limitations of Language

The power of language is further illustrated by the
contrast between Nootka's terms which appear to be
all verbs and our own division between nouns and
verbs; for us, phenomena are divided into those
that change and those that are fixed, but for the
user of Nootka all phenomena are changing. The
impact of language on the user is suggested by the
linguistic relativity hypothesis, which states that
language influences the user to understand the
world in a certain way. For example, the noun
"sociology" or "scientific method" influence us to
see sociology and the scientific method as relatively static, whereas a user of Nootka would tend
to see them as dynamic.

c   What is Culture?

Language is a vital tool for learning culture, which
provides us with an overall blueprint for living.
Culture is a system of widely shared expectations
and goals, or norms and values. There is unity to
culture, that is, the various norms and values are
interrelated. Thus, we speak of it as a "system"
rather than simply a collection of norms and values.
Expectations and goals that are unique to one indiv-

vidual, or that are not widely shared, are not part of culture. Material things like the American flag are not part of culture, but they could not be understood without reference to culture.

d   Expectations and Goals

Expectations are roughly synonymous with thoughts, beliefs, opinions, understandings and speculations. When beliefs or expectations are widely shared, they tend to take on a certain degree of force or pressure, perhaps because of our emphasis on conforming behavior. Goals or interests may be concrete or abstract, and we may be highly aware of them. We may have as a goal the maintenance of something we already have, such as freedom, or a goal may represent something we aspire to. Goals may be relatively specific and trivial, such as an ice cream cone, or quite fundamental, such as equality. A subculture is like a culture (a system of norms and values), except that it is shared primarily within some subgroup of society, such as Italian-Americans.

e   Cultural Differences Illustrated: Germany and the United States

In a study by Townsend comparing attitudes about mental illness in the U.S. and Germany, the differences between Americans and Germans was greater than the differences between lay and professional people in either country. Thus, cultural differences exceeded subcultural ones. For example, Americans emphasized (more than Germans) the worth of individual efforts to solve problems, an approach related to such values as activity and work or achievement and success. Thus, the mental health professional is first an American or German and only second a physician or nurse.

2.3 Ethnocentrism and Cultural Relativism

Ethnocentrism, or seeing the world only through the lens of one's own culture, is found in all societies. It helps to preserve the unity of a given culture, but it is also associated with prejudice against those with a different cultural background from one's own. Cultural relativism, by contrast, is an orientation to viewing others from the perspective of their own culture. Some cultures tend to be less ethnocentric than others. For example, the

16

Hindu concept of <u>darshana</u> or point of view is associated with the idea than many different <u>darshana</u> contribute to an understanding of the larger truth, as represented by <u>Brahman</u>.

2.4   Norms and Values: The Elements of Culture

a   Norms

Norms (widely shared expectations) include folkways (regarded as useful but not essential), mores (regarded as essential), and laws (formally enforced). Only a tiny proportion of norms are laws, illustrating the power of non-legal norms to regulate behavior. The mores in society give us clues as to which values are fundamental. Normative conflict is illustrated by contradictory pieces of advice, such as "Go ahead and enjoy yourself" and "But be careful."

b   Values

Sociologists focus on values (widely shared goals) which are emphasized in society. For example, Williams has developed this listing of the fifteen dominant value orientations in American society: achievement and success, activity and work, moral orientation, humanitarian mores, efficiency and practicality, progress, material comfort, equality, freedom, external conformity, science and secular rationality, nationalism-patriotism, democracy, individual personality, and racism and related group-superiority themes. Values can conflict with one another, as illustrated by the values of equality and racism. Conflicts can be related to neuroses within the individual.

2.5   Culture and Social Organization

A study of membership in organizations reveals that although most Americans do not join several organizations, we tend to join them more than many other peoples. Such joining illustrates our patterns of social organization, as distinct from our culture, granting that the two are interrelated and together make up our social structure. By making such distinctions we are able to point specifically at social relationships as distinct from norms and values.

17

2.6 Cultural and Subcultural Change

a Equality Between the Sexes: Cultural Change

The women's liberation movement in the United
States, with its focus on the achievement of equality,
illustrates the phenomenon of cultural change. For
example, professional schools are opening up more
and more places for women, and women are also making
gains in undergraduate education. At the same time,
women's involvement in property crimes has increased
rapidly in the last decade.

b Community Development: Subcultural Change

Huasahuasi, an agriculturally-based community on
the slopes of the Andes in Peru, experienced rapid
change as a result of a community development project. It was headed by Ulises Moreno, a native of
Huasahuasi who did his doctoral dissertation on
Peruvian potatoes at Cornell University. He was
also able to involve a group of professors and
students from a university in Lima representing
a number of disciplines (such as entomology, sociology, agronomy and economics), and the group dealt
with a wide range of problems in Huasahuasi. In
addition to greatly improving the potato yields
in Huasahuasi, the project was successful in many
other ways, such as helping the community government to expand its responsibilities with an emphasis
on the values of equality and democracy.

SELF-QUIZ

Multiple Choice: In the space provided, enter the letter of the answer that best completes the question.

_____ 1. Biological evolution and biological adaptation are related in that

   a) both have to do with genetic changes over long periods of time
   b) both have to do with cultural change
   c) both have to do with changes in social organization
   d) both have to do with changes in social structure

_____ 2. Language

   a) is a system of widely shared expectations and goals
   b) functions only toward improving human adaptation
   c) is a blueprint or design for living in society
   d) is a system of symbols

_____ 3. The linguistic relativity hypothesis

   a) states that cultures cannot be judged on some absolute scale
   b) states that languages evolve differently, depending on their origins
   c) states that a language influences its users to understand the world in a certain way
   d) states that language provides a blueprint for living in society

_____ 4. The phenomena of culture, according to the text definition,

   a) are intangible or nonmaterial
   b) are largely biological in nature
   c) are largely material
   d) are both material and nonmaterial

_____ 5. Goals and expectations are related in that

   a) they are both elements of social organization
   b) they are both elements of culture

c) they are elements of subculture but not culture
d) they are elements of culture but not sub-culture

_____ 6. If Townsend's comparison of German and American attitudes toward mental health illustrates more general phenomena, then

a) American teachers would tend to be closer to American students in attitudes toward teaching than to German teachers
b) American students would tend to be closer to German students in attitudes toward teaching than the closeness in attitude between American and German teachers
c) American teachers' attitudes toward teaching would be closer to German teachers than to American students
d) none of the above

_____ 7. Cultural relativism is best illustrated by

a) seeing everything in terms of right and wrong
b) practicing what you preach
c) learning foreign languages
d) teaching others the nature of our society

_____ 8. Which of the following is not one of the major value orientations in American society listed by Williams:

a) religion
b) material comfort
c) progress
d) racism and related group-superiority themes

_____ 9. Expectations, goals and social interactions are related in that

a) all are elements of culture (as defined in the text)
b) expectations and goals are elements of culture
c) all are elements of social organization
d) expectations and goals, but not social relationships, are elements of social structure

20

_____ 10. The analysis of community development in Huasahuasi best illustrates the idea that

    a) development depends on focussing on one community problem
    b) cultural change does not affect change in social organization
    c) an interdisciplinary approach does not work in practice
    d) lack of cooperation between large and small farmers can hinder a community development project dealing with agricultural innovation

_____ 11. Biological adaptation is best illustrated by

    a) the women's liberation movement
    b) community development in Huasahuasi
    c) attitudes toward mental health of German professionals
    d) the absence of a particular breeding period for Homo sapiens

_____ 12. If language was more effective in doing what it presently does,

    a) it would consist of symbols that are all nouns
    b) it would enable the individual to apply more of human experiences to any given situation
    c) it would introduce us to the blueprint or design for living in society
    d) it would have no grammar

_____ 13. If we altered our language so that it was very similar to Nootka,

    a) we'd probably see the world in much the same way as we do now
    b) we'd probably see the world in ways similar to the users of Nootka
    c) we'd tend to adopt a static approach to phenomena
    d) none of the above

_____ 14. American culture is best illustrated by

    a) apple pie
    b) the American flag

c) the widespread joining of organizations
d) the widespread desire to make a very good living

_____ 15. Goals are best illustrated by

a) the belief in the existence of God
b) the practice of working 12 hours a day
c) the preference for fancy plumbing over plain plumbing
d) the expectation that the world is heading for disaster

_____ 16. According to Townsend's study of attitudes in the U.S. and Germany,

a) German professionals resemble American lay groups
b) German lay groups resemble American professionals
c) German and American lay groups resemble each other more than German and American professionals
d) German and American professionals resemble each other more than German and American lay groups

_____ 17. The American position of moral absolutism, as discussed by Kaplan,

a) is similar to the Hindu approach to the many darshana
b) illustrates the concept of ethnocentrism
c) is an example of cultural relativism of a special type
d) sharply contrasts with Williams' discussion of the American emphasis on a moral orientation

_____ 18. Mores and folkways

a) are types of laws
b) are types of values
c) are types of societal goals
d) are types of norms

_____ 19. Williams' list of major American value orientations includes

a) religiosity

b) motherhood
c) external conformity
d) recreation

_____ 20. Social organization and culture are related
in that

a) both are elements of social structure
b) they both refer directly to social relationships
c) they both refer directly to norms
d) they both refer directly to values

Concept Recognition: Write the concept or term in the
blank space next to its definition.

_____ 1. A system of expectations and
goals widely shared within a subgroup of society.

_____ 2. Norms formally chosen to be
backed up by punishments for failure to conform to
them, with particular social agencies designated
to do the enforcing.

_____ 3. The system of social relationships within a society or group.

_____ 4. A system of symbols that helps
people communicate past experiences and apply them
to the present.

_____ 5. A tendency to view people's behavior from the perspective of their own culture.

_____ 6. The conflict inherent in values
with opposing goals.

_____ 7. Norms generally regarded as
useful but not essential for society.

_____ 8. Any phenomenon--such as an object, design, or sound--that represents something
other than itself.

_____ 9. A process of change in genetic
makeup from generation to generation.

_____10. Beliefs implying "should" or
"should not".

True/False: Enter "T" for true or "F" for false for the best answer to the statement.

_____ 1. Biological adaptation is illustrated by the development of an opposable thumb in Homo sapiens.

_____ 2. Language is defined as a blueprint or design for living in society.

_____ 3. The different words for snow in Eskimo illustrates the active impact of language on society.

_____ 4. Someone who is conscious of the linguistic relativity hypothesis would tend to be ethnocentric.

_____ 5. A subculture is an element of social organization.

_____ 6. Traditionally, sociologists have tended to study preliterate societies.

_____ 7. According to Townsend's study comparing American and German attitudes, German and American professionals resemble each other more than German and American lay groups.

_____ 8. Mores are illustrated by the expectation that a fork is to be used when eating a salad.

_____ 9. Value conflict in culture is not related to neurotic conflicts within the individual.

_____10. As a result of women's liberation, women's involvement in crime has decreased dramatically.

Concept definition: Write the definition of the concept or term appearing on the left in the blank space next to it.

1. system _____

_____

2. culture _____

_____

3. linguistic relativity hypothesis _____

4. goals _____

5. intelligence _____

6. culture _____

7. norm _____

8. cultural change _____

9. biological adaptation _____

10. ethnocentrism _____

ANSWERS

Self Quiz

1.	a	6.	a	11.	d	16.	c
2.	d	7.	c	12.	b	17.	b
3.	c	8.	a	13.	b	18.	d
4.	a	9.	b	14.	d	19.	c
5.	b	10.	d	15.	c	20.	a

Concept Recognition

1. subculture
2. laws
3. social organization
4. language
5. cultural relativism
6. value conflict
7. folkways
8. symbol
9. biological evolution
10. expectations

True-False

1.	T	6.	F
2.	F	7.	T
3.	T	8.	F
4.	F	9.	F
5.	F	10.	F

Concept Definition

See Glossary in back of this booklet

Socialization

3

OVERVIEW

Human relationships, with the aid of language, enable the individual to see self both as a distinct
object and as an active agent. This socialization process produces the human personality and also carries
culture from one generation to the next. A variety of
concepts help us to understand different aspects of personality structure. Self-image and roles deal with
relatively large units of personality; expectations,
goals and actions have to do with relatively small
units.

SYNOPSIS

3.1 The Nature of Socialization

  a Heredity and Environment

     Within the socialization process, culture is trans-
     mitted to a new generation and the individual under-
     goes profound changes, including the very develop-
     ment of personality. Much of this chapter is given
     over to analyzing the nature of the socialization
     process. To start, both heredity and environment
     are involved. At the turn of the century it was
     thought by many biologists and psychologists, who

27

were generally influenced by Darwin's theory of
biological evolution, that human behavior could
be explained by a large number of instincts or fixed
patterns of behavior for our species. But a variety of studies from anthropology and psychology--
as well as the circular reasoning involved in in-
stinct theories--provided evidence to the contrary.
The importance of human contact in the development
of personality was dramatically demonstrated in
the case of Isabelle, who developed language and
a human personality after a period of isolation up
to the age of six-and-a-half.

b   Formation of the Personality

The process of personality development is partly
explained by Cooley's concept of the looking-glass
self, which refers to the process by which the
reactions of others to us reflect back to us.
Mead, the dominant figure in the sociological understanding of socialization, distinguished between
the individual's unique response to others (the
"I") and his or her organization of the attitudes
of others (the "me"). They work together in phases
to produce both novelty and responsibility, rather
than being pitted against one another inevitably.

c   Symbols and Personality Formation

According to Mead, symbols are crucial to our personality development, and also to our interaction
with others. That interaction is, in fact, symbolic interaction. The Rolls Royce is more than a
car to us: it is a symbol of wealth and power.
That image is created or constituted by us. And
in a similar fashion, we create--through interaction
based on symbols, the human personality.

d   Stages in the Socialization Process

Primary socialization refers to the initial development or construction of the personality, and Mead
focused almost exclusively on this. Continuing
socialization refers to the further modification
of personality--and transmission of culture--beyond
the early years. Whereas the family is, in general,
the key initial agency of socialization, peer groups
as well as the school--and later those at one's
place of work--are important agencies subsequently.
Mead discussed several procedures by which people

28

prepare themselves for taking on future roles (anticipatory socialization). There is the ordinary play of children (such as playing "house") as well as participation in games such as baseball in which explicit rules governing a variety of positions are learned.

e   Resocialization

Sometimes the individual experiences a sharp break with the past, developing his own personality in a way that markedly contrasts with the previous one. The process involved here is that of resocialization. It is illustrated by the experiences of U.N. prisoners of war in Korea. The Chinese began by isolating the prisoners from all those factors that might reinforce their beliefs, goals and self-image: newspapers (other than Chinese newspapers), magazines, radio, mail and visits. Techniques used were repetition (as in lectures), requiring active participation by the prisoner, the insertion of new ideas within old contexts meaningful to the prisoner, rewards and punishments.

3.2   Roles and Self-Image

a   Roles

Words which group individuals together on the basis of common characteristics (poor, rich, educated, uneducated) create social categories. We tend to associate certain ideas with each category, that is, we stereotype people in a given category. For example, "girls" may be thought of as "pretty," "smiling" and "carefree." In this way, values and norms come to be associated with social categories. And roles, or systems of such values and norms, come to be associated with social categories and provide the individual with a script for his or her behavior. As for the actual behavior of the individual in relation to any such script, there is always at least some degree of role taking (behavior in conformity to the script) and role making (behavior rewriting a given script).

b   Self-Image

An individual's set of roles tend to be organized around that person's self-image or overall view of self. An individual, for example, might tend to be subordinate in all or most of his roles. The Twenty-Statements Test is a technique for measuring self-image. People ask themselves "Who am I?" and, in their answers, refer to their social categories as well as their actual role taking and role making behavior. By means of the self-image, the individual achieves unity among these social categories as well as the behavior he or she exhibits in relation to them.

3.3 Expectations, Goals and Actions

a Expectations

The Wizard of Oz illustrates one way of dividing up the human personality; the components here are the head or thinking, the heart or feeling, and the courage to act. This is similar to the division in this Section among expectations, goals and actions. Concerning expectations, these are related to scientific predictions. The scientist tends to use permeable language in making predictions, that is, statements which are undogmatic or open to new information. Unscientific or impermeable language is stereotypical; for example, a bureaucrat is seen as the same as all other bureaucrats or as nothing but a bureaucrat. The Flatlanders of Chapter 1 saw their two-dimensional world in an impermeable way.

b Goals

Freud alerted us to the importance of conflicting goals within the individual that are repressed or buried within the unconscious mind and revealed indirectly by slips of the tongue or bungled actions. Those slips are analogous to the steam escaping from a kettle, with the boiling water analogous to the conflicting goals. Freud alerted us to the importance of becoming aware of those conflicts so that we can deal with them effectively. Sociologists along with some psychoanalysts who followed Freud have pointed to the relationship between value conflicts in society and goal conflicts within the individual.

c Actions

B.F. Skinner is a psychologist who emphasizes how our actions from one moment to the next can be altered on the basis of reinforcements. His Walden

Two is a fictional description of his ideal community, based on "a constantly experimental attitude toward everything." The *Walden Two* tea service, for example, eliminates cups and saucers because of their inefficiency when compared with tall glasses. Sociologists as well as psychologists have used the idea of reinforcement in their work. For example, Kozloff developed a project in which parents of children without speech were taught to socialize their children so as to produce functional speech. He used devices like videotaping their behavior in the home as well as giving role playing demonstrations to alert parents to the kinds of reinforcements they used that maintained the no-speech pattern in their offsprings' behavior as well as the kinds of reinforcements which could improve the situation.

SELF-QUIZ

Multiple Choice: In the space provided, enter the letter of the answer that best completes the question.

_____ 1. Socialization is a process dealing almost exclusively with

    a) learning in school from kindergarten through college
    b) the formation of personality structure in the family setting
    c) the transmission of culture from one generation to the next
    d) the development of personality and the transmission of culture

_____ 2. The story of Isabelle, a child raised in isolation,

    a) illustrates the importance of human contact in the development of speech and personality
    b) illustrates how we cannot compensate for such early deprivation
    c) illustrates the instinctual nature of speech patterns
    d) illustrates none of the above

_____ 3. The concept of the looking-glass self is illustrated by

    a) role taking
    b) role making
    c) learning to see the self as beautiful when others treat us as beautiful
    d) learning to treat others as beautiful when they appear to be beautiful

_____ 4. Mead's "I" differs from his "me" in that

    a) the "I", but not the "me," is based on symbolic interaction
    b) the "me," but not the "I," refers to unique aspects of the self
    c) the "I" gives the sense of freedom, the "me" the sense of responsibility
    d) the "I" is conflict-oriented, the "me" is oriented toward cooperation

5. According to Mead, language is related to personality in that

   a) the personality functions to create language
   b) language enables interaction to create the personality
   c) language and personality are created by roles
   d) both are sharply limited by instincts

6. The generalized other is illustrated by

   a) the perspectives of one's father
   b) the perspectives of one's family as a whole
   c) the perspectives of one's teacher of English
   d) one's own general perspectives on the nature of society

7. Anticipatory and continuing socialization are related in that

   a) both are agencies of socialization functioning primarily in childhood
   b) both function primarily in later life
   c) both lead to changes in the personality
   d) both are mechanisms of resocialization

8. Resocialization and socialization differ in that

   a) we all undergo resocialization, but not socialization
   b) they both tend to occur during the very early years
   c) we all undergo socialization, but not resocialization
   d) they both deal primarily with education in school

9. Role conflict is best illustrated by

   a) the conflict between studying for a midterm exam and basketball practice for the varsity
   b) the conflict between one's childhood and adult roles at different stages in life
   c) the conflict between the "I" and the "me"
   d) none of the above

_____ 10. Roles and social categories are related in that

      a) they both focus on role making
      b) they both refer primarily to the "I"
      c) they both conflict with the individual's self-image
      d) a role provides the script for members of a given social category

_____ 11. Role taking differs from role making in that

      a) the role taker rewrites the script for a role
      b) the role maker behaves in conformity to a role's script
      c) role making is an action, role taking is an expectation
      d) role taking changes a role less than role making

_____ 12. Van Horne's description of his experiences in his first full-time job as a sociologist illustrates the idea that

      a) the pressure for role making can be very high
      b) the pressure før role taking can be very high
      c) the self-image is crucial to any role
      d) anticipatory socialization pays off

_____ 13. The individual's view of self

      a) is his or her self-image
      b) is the "I"
      c) is the "me"
      d) is almost invariably in conflict with the individual's view of others

_____ 14. The Twenty-Statements Test

      a) is a measure of role making
      b) is a measure of role taking
      c) is a measure of the "I"
      d) is a measure of self-image

_____ 15. Personality structure is

      a) the individual's system of expectations,

goals and actions
b) the individual's system of roles organized around a self-image
c) neither of the above
d) both of the above (a and b)

_____ 16. An impermeable usage of language is best illustrated by

a) thinking of Communists as diverse kinds of people
b) thinking of Fascists as nothing but Fascists
c) thinking of the symbolic dimension of language
d) thinking of language rather than what language denotes

_____ 17. Freud was largely concerned with

a) the individual's consciousness
b) the unconscious mind
c) conflicts between cultural values
d) teaching the individual to repress conflicts

_____ 18. The forgetting of names and words, according to Freud,

a) illustrates the operation of hidden conflicts
b) has no rational explanation
c) illustrates conflicts within consciousness
d) is based on the conflict between the "I" and the "me"

_____ 19. In Skinner's Walden Two,

a) people use a scientific approach to human behavior
b) punishment is the fundamental basis for controlling behavior
c) tradition is emphasized
d) all of the above

_____ 20. In dealing with lack of speech in children, Kozloff

a) worked directly with the children in a systematic way
b) was successful in one-third of the cases

c) taught the parents ways of relating to
their children
d) taught the children ways of relating to
their parents

Concept Recognition: Write the concept or term in the
blank space next to its definition.

_____ 1. Behavior in conformity to a
role's script.

_____ 2. Removal from awareness.

_____ 3. The individual's view of self.

_____ 4. Interaction based on symbols.

_____ 5. The process by which the individual develops a personality structure and culture
is transmitted from one generation to the next.

_____ 6. A system of norms and values that
provides the script for a member of a given social
category.

_____ 7. Social structures taking part
in the socialization process.

_____ 8. A usage of a concept so that
there is openness to new information.

_____ 9. Patterns of behavior that are
biologically fixed and universal for a species.

_____10. Contradictory scripts applying
to a given individual.

True/False: Enter "T" for true or "F" for false for the
best answer to the statement.

_____ 1. Socialization is a process that ends in the
early years.

_____ 2. Instinctual theories frequently involve circular reasoning.

_____ 3. The "I" and the "me" are phases of a social
process.

_____ 4. Resocialization is experienced by all of us in

36

all stages of life.

_____ 5. Role conflict refers to the clash between role
          making and role taking.

_____ 6. In role making the individual rewrites a role's
          script.

_____ 7. The Twenty-Questions Test tends to unearth the
          social categories within which the individual
          places himself as well as his role taking and
          role making behavior.

_____ 8. The division of the personality within The
          Wizard of Oz (illustrated by the Scarecrow,
          the Tin Woodman, and the Cowardly Lion)
          parallels the distinctions among expectations,
          goals and action.

_____ 9. Thinking that all racists are alike illus-
          trates permeable usage of language.

_____ 10. In the illustration of the boiling unconscious,
          the boiling water symbolizes the repressed
          conflict.

Concept definition: Write the definition of the concept
or term appearing on the left in the blank space next to
it.

1. I _____

_____

2. expectation _____

_____

3. social categories _____

_____

4. resocialization _____

_____

5. personality structure _____

_____

6. me _____

_____

7. generalized other _____

_____

8. looking-glass self _____

_____

9. personality structure _____

_____

10. continuing socialization _____

_____

ANSWERS

Self Quiz

1.	d	6.	b	11.	d	16.	b
2.	a	7.	c	12.	b	17.	b
3.	c	8.	c	13.	a	18.	a
4.	c	9.	a	14.	d	19.	a
5.	b	10.	d	15.	d	20.	c

Concept Recognition

1. role taking
2. repression
3. self-image
4. symbolic interaction
5. socialization
6. role
7. agencies of socialization
8. permeable usage
9. instincts
10. role conflict

True-False

1.	F	6.	T
2.	T	7.	T
3.	T	8.	T
4.	F	9.	F
5.	F	10.	T

Concept Definition

See Glossary in back of this booklet

Conforming and Deviant Behavior

4

OVERVIEW

Conforming to group norms and values is a way of adjusting to society, but it can also create problems, as illustrated by Lt. William Calley's massacre of civilians at My Lai. Correspondingly, deviant behavior not only can create problems but also can be an adjustment procedure. For example, individuals labeled by others as delinquents can come to define themselves in the same way and then adjust their behavior to match that self-image. Language plays a crucial role in both conforming and deviant behavior, for it provides the tools people use to define situations as well as themselves.

SYNOPSIS

4.1 Conforming Behavior (conforming behavior, deviant behavior)

a   Conforming Behavior as a Way of Solving Problems

It is exceedingly difficult to conceive of society without a good deal of behavior that conforms to existing norms and values; indeed, the terms "norm" and "value" are defined on the basis of phenomena that are widely shared. Beyond the general importance of a fair measure of conformity

for society, there are particular uses to which
conforming behavior is put, such as the formation
of groups like Alcoholics Anonymous in which group
pressure supports the desires of the individual.
This understanding of the functions of conformity
for society contrasts with Freud's emphasis on an
inevitable conflict between the individual and
society; it is much closer to Mead's orientation
(presented in Chapter 3). De Sica's Umberto D,
with its portrayal of Umberto's attachment to his
dog as helping him to find a reason for living,
provides an illustration of the power of conforming
behavior.

b   Conforming Behavior as a Way of Creating Problems

Despite the importance of conforming behavior for
society, such behavior also creates serious problems. The Asch experiment shows how readily people
conform to the expectations of others (as they understand or perceive them). Such conformity not only
can distort the actions an individual takes or the
individual's faith in his or her own perception
but the individual's actual perception as well.
The Milgram experiment shows to what lengths an
individual might go in conforming to an authority
figure: sending what he or she believes might
easily be a lethal dose of electricity to an unwilling subject. The closer such individuals were
to the subject in the electric chair, the less willing they were to follow orders. Such extreme behavior would not occur, according to many individuals who attempted to predict the experimental
results.

c   Conforming Behavior and Language

Lt. William Calley classified civilian men, women
and children at My Lai as enemy soldiers, laying
the basis for killing them. This illustrates the
influence which a "definition of the situation" has
on our subsequent behavior. Such definitions are
analogous to several stages of the scientific method:
defining a problem, constructing hypotheses and
drawing conclusions. Also, they have to do with
several elementary units of the individual's behavior (expectations and goals); thus, they function
from moment to moment in everyday life. Euphemisms
like "pacification," which are relatively impermeable
(not open to much information), illustrate ways in

40

which authority figures attempt to gain support
for certain definitions of the situation.

4.2 Deviant Behavior

a Deviant Behavior as a Way of Creating Problems

Deviant behavior, such as the autism of children
illustrated in Sociological Practice 3-1, can create problems for the individual and society. Crime
is a more widespread example, and mental illness is
another. Durkheim's analysis of suicide suggests
the importance of close social relationships in
deterring suicide.

b Deviant Behavior as a Way of Solving Problems

Merton has argued that society's emphasis on monetary success puts tremendous pressure on poor or
uneducated people to find illegitimate means (such
as crime) for attaining this cultural value. Of
course, this "solution" to their problem creates
other problems. The Bicycle Thief illustrates crime
as a solution to the problem of feeding one's family.
Yet we should understand that crime is a phenomenon
that occurs among the well-to-do as well as the poor.
Such white-collar criminals generally have less
chance of being jailed because, for example, they
can afford to engage in legal battles.

c Deviant Behavior and Language

Language is a powerful force that can influence the
development of deviant behavior. This is illustrated by a deviance amplification process within
which the individual learns to see self as a delinquent more and more as he or she engages in ever
more lawbreaking behavior. Such deviance partially
caused by self-image as a deviant is called "secondary deviation." Another illustration of the power
of language is the "self-fulfilling prophesy," such
as the student who is able to pass an examination
but, convinced that he will fail, proceeds to fail.
Here, a definition of the situation that is originally false becomes true. Or a government, convinced that another government plans to start a war
(even though that is not true), proceeds to start
the war itself. Such self-fulfilling prophesies are
based on certain definitions of the situation.

41

4.3 Crime

a The Nature of Crime

Crime is only one small portion of deviant behavior,
namely, deviance in violation of law. Law itself
is based on culture, such as the Ten Commandments.

b Society's Reactions to Crime

A number of principles generally are involved in
the reactions of contemporary societies to crime,
such as retaliation, rehabilitation, protection
(of the members of society) and deterrence.

c Some Causes of Crime

One key sociological insight into the origins of
crime is that such behavior frequently represents
conformity to the norms and values within a criminal subculture. Thus, deviance from the laws and
norms of society may be conformity to the norms of
a subculture. Such subcultures arise in relation
to the fundamental values and norms within the culture as a whole. For example--following Merton's
ideas--a society emphasizing economic success yet
erecting barriers (for many people) to the legitimate attainment of such success encourages the
origin of such subcultures. In analyzing the causes
of crime, we must be careful not to lump different
kinds of crime together. For example, Richard
Helms' refusal to testify fully to a Senate committee (resulting in a $2,000 fine) about the oper-
ations of the C.I.A. in Chile is quite different
from the crimes of Al Capone.

d Crime and Self-Image

Just as an individual's self-image as a delinquent
can, through a process of deviance amplification,
work to produce secondary deviation, so can the
reverse occur. Specifically, a self-image as law-
abiding can, through a process of deviance counteraction, continue to help the individual avoid break-
ing the law, and this in turn will further strengthen
that self-image.

e Criminals and Victims

Crime is very often a social interaction and, as

such, involves the behavior of a victim as well
as that of a lawbreaker. Studies show that many
victims contribute to a greater or lesser degree
in the crimes perpetrated on them. For example,
a study in Philadelphia reveals that about one-
quarter of homicides were precipitated by the victim. In addition to a victim's being the first to
strike a blow or draw a deadly weapon, he may help
to originate a crime against himself through simple
passivity or active incitement. Bystanders frequently affect the onset of crime, as in the case
of the murder of Kitty Genovese whose screams were
unheeded by the thirty-eight people who heard her
for a half-hour period. In one experimental study,
most people went to investigate taped screams from
an adjoining room, but individuals paired with someone instructed to ignore the screams almost uni-
formly ignored them.

SELF-QUIZ

Multiple Choice: In the space provided, enter the letter of the answer that best completes the question.

_____ 1. Weight Watchers groups are probably effective largely because

     a) deviants like to get together
     b) they exert strong pressures on members to conform to their norms
     c) they are experts in facilitating deviance amplification
     d) the people involved generally know one another socially

_____ 2. Umberto D's avoidance of suicide illustrates Durkheim's idea that

     a) a dog is man's best friend
     b) social relationships with pets deter suicide
     c) close social relationships can tend to prevent suicide
     d) unmarried men with pets have fewer suicides than married men without pets

_____ 3. In the Asch experiment, distortion of perception involved

     a) conformity because people doubted their own perceptive processes
     b) conformity without awareness that one's estimates were distorted by group pressure
     c) conformity in order to avoid appearing different or inferior
     d) none of the above

_____ 4. In the Milgram experiment, audiences of adults and students

     a) incorrectly predicted that many of the subjects would administer 450 volts
     b) correctly predicted that many of the subjects would administer 450 volts
     c) incorrectly predicted that none of the subjects would reach 450 volts
     d) correctly predicted that none of the subjects would reach 450 volts

_____ 5. In variations of the Milgram experiment,

a) the laboratory was supposedly owned by Harvard rather than Yale
b) a pet poodle was tied on a leash next to the experimenter
c) the "learner" was a dog and barked instead of screaming
d) the subject's proximity to the "learner" was altered

_____ 6. The definition of the situation is analogous to

a) only testing hypotheses within the scientific method
b) defining a problem, constructing hypotheses and drawing conclusions within the scientific method
c) only defining a problem within the scientific method
d) only constructing hypotheses within the scientific method

_____ 7. An illustration of a relatively impermeable usage of language is

a) whore
b) traitor
c) neither of the above
d) both (a) and (b)

_____ 8. Labelling the bombing of villages "pacification" best illustrates

a) deviance amplification
b) deviance counteraction
c) Durkheim's hypothesis
d) impermeable language

_____ 9. Lawbreaking and suicide are related in that both are excellent illustrations of

a) deviant behavior
b) deviance counteraction
c) conforming behavior
d) impermeable language

_____ 10. According to Merton, lawbreaking is encouraged by a society which

a) stresses monetary success and blocks legitimate channels to it

45

b) does not stress monetary success and blocks legitimate channels to it
c) stresses monetary success and opens legitimate channels to it
d) does not stress monetary success and opens legitimate channels to it

_____ 11. In The Bicycle Thief, the theft best illustrates

a) legitimate channels to illegitimate ends
b) legitimate channels to legitimate ends
c) illegitimate channels to illegitimate ends
d) illegitimate channels to legitimate ends

_____ 12. Forgery and embezzlement best illustrate

a) white collar crime
b) deviance amplification
c) deviance counteraction
d) secondary deviation

_____ 13. A community's labelling of an individual as a delinquent

a) can easily lead to secondary deviation
b) is related to the process of deviance amplification
c) is not a good illustration of deviance counteraction
d) all of the above

_____ 14. A mutual-causal relationship is related to deviance amplification in that

a) deviance amplification may or may not be a mutual-causal relationship
b) a mutual-causal relationship may or may not be deviance amplification
c) both may produce deviance counteraction
d) both are caused by a third factor

_____ 15. The self-fulfilling prophesy

a) refers to an initially true definition of the situation
b) refers to an initially false definition of the situation
c) does not refer to a definition of the situation
d) evokes behavior that falsifies the initial

46

conception

_____ 16. Crime is best illustrated by

    a) the violation of law
    b) deviance from folkways
    c) deviance from norms
    d) deviance amplification

_____ 17. The principle of retaliation

    a) is almost the same as the principle of
       deterrence
    b) is based on a balance-scale image of jus-
       tice
    c) has been abandoned in modern society
    d) none of the above

_____ 18. A major cause of crime is

    a) conforming to a deviant subculture
    b) deviating from a deviant subculture
    c) normative "aberration"
    d) deviance counteraction

_____ 19. The Richard Helms case, in which he failed to
        testify "fully and accurately" before a Senate
        committee,

    a) illustrates deviance from legal norms
    b) illustrates conformity to norms within the
       C.I.A.
    c) both of the above
    d) neither (a) nor (b)

_____ 20. The 1964 murder of Kitty Genovese best illus-
        trates

    a) passivity of the victim
    b) victim-instigated crime
    c) bystander apathy
    d) deviance counteraction

Concept Recognition: Write the concept or term in the
blank space next to its definition.

_____ 1. A false definition of the situation evoking a new behavior which makes the
originally false conception come true.

_____ 2. Behavior falling outside the
acceptable range according to societal or group
norms and values.

_____ 3. A mutual-causal relationship
producing decreasing deviance.

_____ 4. The shaping of behavior through
interpreting the past and outlining future directions.

_____ 5. That portion of deviant behavior
which is in violation of existing laws.

_____ 6. A relationship between two factors in which each continues to affect the other.

_____ 7. Behavior falling inside the
acceptable range according to societal or group
norms and values.

_____ 8. Assign to a social category.

_____ 9. Deviance partially caused by
the individual's self-image as a deviant.

_____10. A mutual-causal relationship
producing increasing deviance.

True/False: Enter "T" for true or "F" for false for the
best answer to the statement.

_____ 1. In the Asch experiment, distortion of judg-
           ment involved subjects' doubting their own
           perceptive processes.

_____ 2. In the Milgram experiment, the closer the sub-
           jects were to the "learner," the greater their
           conformity to experimenter orders.

_____ 3. William I. Thomas introduced the concept of
           "definition of the situation."

_____ 4. An impermeable usage of language illustrates
           scientific usage.

_____ 5. White collar crime is illustrated by the crim-
           inal career of Al Capone who used violence
           effectively to achieve his ends.

_____ 6. Deviance amplification is a mutual-causal relationship.

_____ 7. Deviance counteraction is a mutual-causal relationship.

_____ 8. Secondary deviance is related to the deviant's
self-image.

_____ 9. A self-fulfilling prophesy is a prediction
that has no effect on what actually occurs.

_____10. There is solid evidence that victims frequently
help to produce the crimes against themselves.

Concept Definition: Write the definition of the concept
or term appearing on the left in the blank space next
to it.

1. definition of the situation _____

_____

2. conforming behavior _____

_____

3. label _____

_____

4. deviance amplification _____

_____

5. self-fulfilling prophesy _____

_____

6. mutual-causal relationship _____

_____

7. deviant behavior _____

_____

8. secondary deviation _____

_____

9. crime _____

_____

10. deviance counteraction _____

_____

ANSWERS

Self Quiz

1.	b	6.	b	11.	d	16.	a
2.	c	7.	d	12.	a	17.	b
3.	b	8.	d	13.	d	18.	a
4.	c	9.	a	14.	b	19.	c
5.	d	10.	a	15.	b	20.	c

Concept Recognition

1. self-fulfilling prophesy
2. deviant behavior
3. deviance counteraction
4. definition of the situation
5. crime
6. mutual-causal relationship
7. conforming behavior
8. label
9. secondary deviation
10. deviance amplification

True-False

1.	T	6.	T
2.	F	7.	T
3.	T	8.	T
4.	F	9.	F
5.	F	10.	T

Concept Definition

See Glossary in back of this booklet

Sociological Theory

5

OVERVIEW

There are five major theoretical orientations in
sociology. When used together, such as in the analysis
of Joan of Arc's struggle to defeat the English and
crown a French king, they can capture many of the com-
plexities of human behavior. Structural-functionalism
and conflict theory focus on society as a whole. Symbolic interactionism, ethnomethodology, and exchange
theory center on the individual within the small group.
However, there is considerable overlapping among these
orientations. Readers should be warned that the text--
for reasons of space--presents each one in a simplified
form. Along with each orientation, there is a set of
concepts which comprise its tools for analysis.

SYNOPSIS

5.1 Introduction to Sociological Theory

   a The Nature of Theory

   "Theory" is used in several ways by sociologists.
   It can refer to a system of hypotheses or concepts
   or, when used more loosely, to a single concept or
   hypothesis. Theory is fundamental to every stage
   of the scientific method. Each new piece of research must be placed within the context of previous

research in that general area, and theory helps the investigator do this. The theory behind any new research is stated, and it is related to the existing theory bearing on the topic being investigated.

b   Major Theoretical Orientations

There are hundreds and thousands of theories in sociology. However, we can view them as clustering around a small number of major theoretical orientations. Currently, there are five such orientations in sociology: structural-functionalism, conflict theory, symbolic interactionism, exchange theory, and ethnomethodology. We should approach these orientations cautiously. We should not blind ourselves to the complexity and diversity of the theories they encompass. Also, we should not forget that sociological theories and major theoretical orientations continue to change. Further, there is considerable overlap among these orientations. Bearing these qualifications in mind: (1) structural-functionalism centers on existing patterns in society as a whole; (2) conflict theory emphasizes change in society as a whole; (3) symbolic interactionism and (4) exchange theory focus on existing patterns in small groups and also deal with the individual and (5) ethnomethodology centers on change in small groups as well as the individual.

5.2   Structural-Functionalism

Structural-functionalism is the most influential of sociology's theoretical orientations. Its focus is on the contributions made to society as a whole by groups or social structures. For example, how does any group's activities help with the continuing existence of society? How does seemingly negative activities, like crime or mental illness, nevertheless make such contributions or have such functions? Conversely, structural-functionalism covers negative consequences (dysfunctions) for society, that is consequences lessening society's ability to adapt or even threatening society's very existence. Some functions and dysfunctions are intended by those involved as well as obvious to them (manifest), and others are neither intended nor recognized (latent).

5.3 Conflict Theory

Conflict theory is not oriented to explaining the continuation of society as is structural-functionalism. Rather it is directed at examining opposition or conflict in society and the changes that result. Karl Marx, the most well-known theorist with this orientation, centered on the conflict between owners and workers in industrial society. He believed that this conflict would become increasingly severe due in part to limited material resources (scarcity). Georg Simmel centered on conflicts in small groups. He believed that all groups exhibit both cooperation and conflict, and he felt that conflict has essential functions for the continuation of the group. The conflict between feudalism and Catholicism (represented by Warwick and Cauchon) and nationalism as well as the prelude to Protestantism (represented by Charles and Joan) from Saint Joan illustrates conflict theory. Conflict theory raises basic questions about the continuation of existing social structures such as feudalism.

5.4 Symbolic Interactionism

In shifting to symbolic interactionism we shift from an emphasis on society as a whole to one on the small group. We might classify symbolic interactionism into three levels of analysis: (1) a level close to the situation, as illustrated by Thomas' focus on the definition of the situation; (2) a level close to the fundamental components of personality structure, as illustrated by the work of Cooley and Mead on the nature of the personality; and (3) an intermediate level centering on the concept of role, as exemplified by the work of Goffman. Thus, symbolic interactionism deals with definitions of the situation, self-image and roles. Goffman's work is illustrated by the concept of "role distance," which refers to the degree of resistance which the individual puts up against a given role. For example, a worker may become overly formal with his or her boss. Shaw's Saint Joan can be used to illustrate the symbolic interactionist orientation. For example, Joan helps Charles to shift his own definition of his situation, including his self-image. He learns to see himself as someone who can take decisive action to drive the English out of France, instead of seeing himself as a coward. This shift involves changes in his self-image as well as in the number of roles he plays.

5.5 Exchange Theory

Just as in the case of symbolic interactionism, there are three different levels of analysis with respect to exchange theory: (1) the level of large-scale social structures, illustrated by the work of Blau; (2) a level very close to the details of any given situation, as illustrated by the work of the structured exchange theorists; and (3) an intermediate level, as exemplified by the work of Homans. Exchange theory focuses on the balance of profits and losses, or rewards and punishments (positive and negative reinforcements) in any given situation. To illustrate from Saint Joan, Joan gives Charles the chance to become a great king as well as become financially secure, thus alerting him to positive reinforcements awaiting him. And if he refuses to follow Joan's advice, Joan--and perhaps God as well--will consider him to be a coward. Similarly, Joan herself has much to gain if she succeeds in driving the English out of France: she will be following the dictates of God and helping to establish a legitimate king for her beloved France.

5.6 Ethnomethodology

Ethnomethodology is the newest of sociology's major theoretical orientations. Its focus is on detailed analysis of situations with particular attention to how people come to define them and, as a consequence, construct or shape reality. Social structure is seen as the resultant of a continuing process in which people define and redefine the situation. Thus, it is potentially highly unstable because it is subject to constant revision. Ethnomethodology originated in the analysis by Garfinkel of jury deliberations. It combines a focus on ordinary people (rather than scientists or specialists) in their everyday interactions ("ethno") with a focus on techniques for solving problems ("methodology"). Accounts are our everyday or common-sense attempts to explain past occurrences, and ethnotheories are common-sense theories about how to solve problems. Ethnotheories often conflict with scientific theories, as illustrated in Sociological Practice 5-1 (Ethnotheories as Substitute Cures).

SELF-QUIZ

Multiple Choice: In the space provided, enter the letter of the answer that best completes the question.

_____ 1. Theory and hypotheses are related in that

   a) a theory may include a number of hypotheses
   b) an hypothesis is more certain than a theory
   c) a concept generally includes a number of theories
   d) a concept generally includes a number of hypotheses

_____ 2. A theory is valuable

   a) for defining problems
   b) for testing hypotheses
   c) both of the above
   d) neither (a) nor (b)

_____ 3. Major theoretical orientations are related to theories in that

   a) each theory generally includes a large number of major theoretical orientations
   b) each major theoretical orientation generally includes a large number of theories
   c) major theoretical orientations are more tentative than theories
   d) theories are more practical than major theoretical orientations

_____ 4. With respect to the major theoretical orientations presented,

   a) they overlap with one another
   b) they were all developed at approximately the same time
   c) they cannot be used at the same time on a given problem
   d) they do not conflict with one another in the least

_____ 5. Which theoretical orientation centers on change and on the individual within the small group:

   a) conflict theory
   b) structural-functionalism
   c) symbolic interactionism

55

d) ethnomethodology

6. The argument that the authority of the king will tend to replace the authority of the aristocracy if he contributes more to society

   a) draws primarily on conflict theory
   b) draws primarily on symbolic interactionism
   c) draws primarily on structural-functionalism
   d) draws primarily on ethnomethodology

7. Latent functions differ from manifest dysfunctions in that

   a) they are at different levels of awareness or recognition
   b) they differ in whether or not they are intended
   c) they differ in whether or not they contribute to society
   d) all of the above

8. Which major theoretical orientation is most concerned with the question: "How is the continuing existence of society to be explained?"

   a) conflict theory
   b) structural-functionalism
   c) exchange theory
   d) symbolic interactionism

9. Marx believed that

   a) the bourgeoisie created very little in the way of productive forces
   b) in industrial society the strength of the proletariat tends to become less and less
   c) the proletariat receive less and less as the bourgeoisie receive more and more
   d) over a period of time, the conflict between the bourgeoisie and the proletariat will become less severe

10. Simmel, who studied conflict in small groups, believed that

   a) social conflict has important functions for a group
   b) social conflict is almost completely dysfunctional for a group

c) cooperation is not essential for a group
d) people would want to continue in their social relationships even if there were no possibility of rebelling against them

_____ 11. Role distance is best illustrated by

a) a private who salutes a captain in the army
b) a private who salutes a captain in a very half-hearted way
c) a surgeon who performs a successful operation, but the patient dies 3 days later
d) a cab-driver who stops at a red light

_____ 12. Symbolic interactionism deals with which concept most directly:

a) accounts
b) ethnotheories
c) roles
d) constructing reality

_____ 13. Which theorists are most closely associated with symbolic interactionism:

a) Dahrendorf and Skinner
b) Thomas and Cooley
c) Garfinkel and Blau
d) Homans and Emerson

_____ 14. Exchange theory is best illustrated by

a) a focus on constructing reality
b) a concern with dysfunctions
c) an emphasis on accounts
d) stress on psychic profits

_____ 15. Which among these exchange theorists are most concerned with reinforcers:

a) Blau
b) Homans
c) Emerson
d) the structured exchange theorists

_____ 16. In an exchange relationship between two people,

a) if one party makes a profit, the other must undergo a loss

b) in any exchange, both parties undergo a loss
c) in an exchange, both parties can easily make a profit
d) none of the above

_____ 17. In Shaw's Epilogue to Saint Joan,

a) Cauchon and Warwick define the situation so that Joan is now invited to return to earth
b) Cauchon defines the situation as in (a), but not Warwick
c) Warwick defines the situation as in (a), but not Cauchon
d) Cauchon and Warwick define the situation so that Joan is not invited to return to earth

_____ 18. A definition of the situation

a) interprets the past and outlines future directions
b) neither interprets the past nor outlines future directions
c) interprets the past but does not outline future directions
d) outlines future directions but does not interpret the past

_____ 19. Ethnomethodology originated in the study of

a) behavior on the beach at Coney Island
b) the private behavior of two justices of the U.S. Supreme Court
c) tape recordings of jury deliberations
d) tape recordings of Star Trek

_____ 20. Which one of these does not illustrate an ethnotheory that has been put forward as a substitute cure, as described in Stimson's analysis of organizational efforts to solve problems:

a) immediate action is needed
b) a thorough scientific study, as well as a detailed examination of all of the relevant research findings, are required
c) just ask those living in the situation
d) human beings are materialistic

Concept Recognition: Write the concept or term in the blank space next to its definition.

_____ 1. A theoretical orientation focusing on the individual's definition of the situation, roles and self-image.

_____ 2. One or more tentative ideas, concepts or statements about the nature of reality or about how to solve a problem.

_____ 3. Limitations on resources for achieving goals or fulfilling values.

_____ 4. A common-sense explanation for past occurrences.

_____ 5. A theoretical orientation emphasizing the opposition among individuals, groups or social structures.

_____ 6. A social structure's consequences for society which lessen society's adaptation or adjustment.

_____ 7. A theoretical orientation emphasizing the goals, rewards and punishments associated with interaction.

_____ 8. A theoretical orientation emphasizing the functions or contributions made to society by existing structures.

_____ 9. Functions which are neither intended nor recognized.

_____10. Degree of resistance against, or disaffection for, a role.

True/False: Enter "T" for true or "F" for false for the best answer to the statement.

_____ 1. Structural-functionalism centers on existing patterns in society.

_____ 2. Functions lessen society's adaptation or adjustment.

_____ 3. Much of conflict theory is based on the assumption of scarcity.

_____ 4. Marx emphasized the importance of collective bargaining for resolving conflicts between owners and workers.

_____ 5. Goffman is primarily an ethnomethodologist.

_____ 6. Cooley and Mead emphasized the concept, "definition of the situation."

_____ 7. Reinforcers can be intangible as well as tangible.

_____ 8. Exchange theory includes theory dealing with large-scale social structures.

_____ 9. Ethnomethodology centers on people's everyday interactions.

_____10. Ethnotheories focus on the future.

Concept Definition: Write the definition of the concept or term appearing on the left in the blank space next to it.

1. manifest functions _____

_____

2. constructing reality _____

_____

3. ethnotheory _____

_____

4. resource _____

_____

5. ethnomethodology _____

_____

6. reinforcers _____

_____

7. functions _____

_____

8. structured exchange _____

_____

9. proletariat _____

_____

10. major theoretical orientation _____

_____

ANSWERS

Self Quiz

1.	a	6.	c	11.	b	16.	c
2.	c	7.	d	12.	c	17.	d
3.	b	8.	b	13.	b	18.	a
4.	a	9.	c	14.	d	19.	c
5.	d	10.	a	15.	d	20.	b

Concept Recognition

1. symbolic interactionism
2. theory
3. scarcity
4. account
5. conflict theory
6. dysfunction
7. exchange theory
8. structural-functionalism
9. latent functions
10. role distance

True-False

1.	T	6.	F
2.	F	7.	T
3.	T	8.	T
4.	F	9.	T
5.	F	10.	T

Concept Definition

See Glossary in back of this booklet

Methods of Sociological Research

6

OVERVIEW

Our ordinary everyday procedures for explaining
phenomena can be quite nonscientific. For example, we
might use biased language, causal oversimplification,
circular reasoning, proof by selected instances, and
non sequitors. By contrast, the scientific method provides for the careful construction and rigorous testing
of hypotheses. These hypotheses stem from existing
theory within the discipline, as illustrated by the
author's study of maladjustment among older people. The
conclusions drawn suggest further problems for investigation in a never-ending process.

SYNOPSIS

6.1   The Aims of Investigation

  a   The Sociology of Knowledge

      The film Rashomon suggests that every individual's
      perception of truth is colored by his or her social,
      historical and personal situation. Karl Mannheim
      was very influential in the origins of sociology
      of knowledge, which studies the relationship be-
      tween the knowledge people collect and the social
      structures surrounding those efforts. He believed
      that scientists can never be completely objective

or arrive at perfect truth. However, at least they can continue to improve their knowledge by examining an ever wider range of ideas and evidence. The idea of research triangulation (the use of multiple theories or methods of investigation) captures Mannheim's orientation. For example, sociologists might employ conflict theory, structural-functionalism, exchange theory, ethnomethodology, and symbolic interactionism. Also, they might make use of surveys, available information, experiments and observation. Such an approach contrasts sharply with the use of a single theory or major theoretical orientation, or of a single research procedure.

b   Nonscientific Ethnotheories and Accounts

Commonsense theories or ethnotheories are used by all of us, yet they frequently are highly misleading in our efforts to develop knowledge. For example, they can teach us to use biased language, to jump to hasty conclusions or generalizations, to oversimplify the causal relationships among phenomena, and to employ circular reasoning. The scientific method teaches us, instead, to use terms that are not emotionally loaded in one direction, to take the time to test ideas against the available evidence, to assume that more causes for a given phenomenon exist than we are able to identify, and to use operational as well as verbal definitions. Commonsense explanations or accounts can be misleading as well. To illustrate, they can involve proof by selected instances, post hoc reasoning, non sequitors and the fallacy of concurrency. By contrast, we can learn from the scientific method to employ sampling procedures (such as probability sampling), to use evidence for assessing whether in fact an event preceding another actually is a cause of it, to use logical reasoning, and to avoid claiming one event causes another simply because they occur at the same time.

6.2   Defining a Research Problem

My own research on how to explain why some older individuals are able to adjust to everyday life far better than others can serve to illustrate the different stages of the scientific method. The definition of a problem--usually the first stage--involves: (1) specifying a particular focus of interest (such as this), (2) statements about the concepts or theories to be used, and (3) statements about the general procedures to be employed in collecting evidence. For example, I was interested in the effect of employment status (independent variable) on degree of adjustment (dependent variable). Also, I was interested in analyzing the results of two interview surveys that had already been performed and recorded on punched cards. In those surveys, probability sampling procedures--which made it possible to draw conclusions to the relatively large populations from which the samples were drawn-- were used.

6.3   Constructing Hypotheses

On the basis of the above definition of the problem, one specific hypothesis was that a greater proportion of retired individuals are maladjusted than employed individuals. Another hypothesis was that older people who identify as middle-aged have a better chance of avoiding maladjustment than older people who identify as old. In order to prepare such hypotheses for testing, it is important to define the concepts or variables involved operationally (develop specific procedures for measuring them). Sociologists employ a number of criteria for developing operational definitions. Most important, efforts are required to develop valid measurements (close correspondence between the measurement and the variable it's supposed to measure). For a measurement to be highly reliable, it must be quite stable over time and consistent across different situations. Precise measurement is measurement that is accurate, or can detect minute differences with respect to the variable. Scaling procedures are sometimes employed to help achieve such precision. Such procedures result in scales, that is, measurements with numerical properties.

6.4   Collecting Evidence for Testing Hypotheses

In the illustration of my own research, the procedure for collecting evidence was the use of available data or previously recorded information. That procedure is also illustrated by Durkheim's investigation of suicide (Section 1.4). Interview and questionnaire surveys are most important tools of the sociologist. The former is illustrated by the survey on which the study of older individuals in this chapter is based. The latter is illustrated

64

by the study of cultural differences between Germany and the U.S. (Section 2.2). Observational procedures for collecting evidence fall into two general types: the informal recording of descriptions, and the systematic recording of descriptions designed to test particular hypotheses. To illustrate, Mead's informal observations within his own family helped him to develop his theory of socialization (Section 3.1). Another technique for collecting evidence is the experiment, in which the investigator actively changes a situation and systematically records the results. For example, the situation before and after the change takes place is compared. Control procedures are used to prevent the interference of outside factors with the hypotheses being tested.

6.5 Analysis and Conclusions

a Statistical Tests of Hypotheses

Results of the analysis of the survey described in Chapter 6 indicate: (1) employment status is related to degree of adjustment; (2) marital status (married or widowed) is related to degree of adjustment; and (3) age identification (self-image as middle-aged or old) is related to degree of adjustment. These three relationships are all "statistically significant at the .01 level." In other words, the chances are about one in a hundred that these relationships do not actually exist within the population that was sampled. In other words, we can be fairly sure that if (for example) a greater proportion of retired individuals than employed individuals in the sample are maladjusted, then the same result is true for the larger population.

b Directions for Future Research

Every study results in certain findings, and those findings in turn suggest directions for future studies. For example, exactly why do those older people who are retired, have lost a spouse, or think of themselves as old tend to be maladjusted? By what process do they become maladjusted? Major theoretical orientations frequently can provide possible answers, laying the basis for additional hypotheses which might be tested. For example, exchange theory alerts us to examine the overall

Fitz Memorial Library

Endicott College
Beverly, Massachusetts 01915

47511

balance of positive and negative reinforcers associated with any given role change or change in
self-image.

Multiple Choice: In the space provided, enter the letter
of the answer that best completes the question.

_____   1. The sociology of knowledge

a) emphasizes statistical procedures for obtaining knowledge
b) centers on how knowledge is applied to
   solve problems
c) centers on the relations among different
   bits of knowledge
d) stresses the relationship between knowledge
   collected and the social structures involved
   in such efforts

_____   2. Evidence and objectivity are related in that

a) both focus on obtaining knowledge as to the
   nature of reality
b) both are approaches for combatting bias
c) neither a) nor b) are correct
d) both a) and b) are correct

_____   3. Research triangulation is illustrated by

a) using quantitative procedures
b) using interviewing techniques
c) using experiments
d) using structural-functionalism and conflict
   theory

_____   4. Circular reasoning is illustrated by

a) defining terms in such a way that they
   can't be proven wrong
b) focusing on only one cause within a complex
   phenomenon
c) basing a general hypothesis on scanty information
d) being unable to imagine a contradiction to
   one's preconceived ideas

_____   5. The fallacy of composition is illustrated by

a) assuming that if compulsory retirement is
   functional for society, it is functional
   for organizations within society
b) assuming that if compulsory retirement is

functional for an organization, it is functional for society as a whole
c) claiming that because event B follows A
that event A is a cause of event B
d) claiming that because events A and B occur
at the same time, that one is a cause of
the other

_____ 6. Karl Mannheim, in his approach to the sociology
of knowledge, believed that

a) scientists will always be biased to a degree
b) perfect truth can be achieved by scientists
c) each social scientist should focus on a
small number of ideas in order to develop
them well and not range too widely
d) Marxist theory should serve as the foundation for the sociology of knowledge

_____ 7. In which of these hypotheses is degree of adjustment the only dependent variable:

a) retirement affects degree of adjustment
and self-image
b) degree of adjustment affects self-image
c) degree of adjustment is affected by self-
image
d) degree of adjustment affects retirement and
self-image

_____ 8. With regard to probability sampling,

a) this is a procedure that generally is used
to obtain a proof by selected instances
b) it is a procedure guaranteeing no error in
generalizing from the sample to the population
c) it's a sampling procedure in which each unit
has a known probability of being chosen
d) it's a sampling procedure in which the
chance of error is no greater than 5 in 100

_____ 9. One of the hypotheses in the study described
in Chapter 6 is:

a) older people who identify as middle-aged are
more maladjusted than older people who
identify as old
b) the chances for maladjustment are greater
for those older individuals undergoing im-

portant role changes than among those who
are not
c) a greater proportion of employed individuals
are maladjusted than retired invididuals
d) a greater proportion of married than widowed
people are maladjusted

_____ 10. Reliability of measurement is illustrated by

a) a broken scale that continues to give the
same reading
b) a scale that gives the correct weight two
out of three times
c) both of the above
d) neither a) nor b)

_____ 11. Validity, reliability and precision are related
in that

a) a measure may be reliable without being
precise
b) a measure may be reliable without being
valid
c) both of the above
d) neither of the above

_____ 12. An operational definition of degree of adjustment is illustrated by

a) a series of items on an interview schedule
used to form a scale of adjustment
b) an abstract definition based on research
in the area
c) an abstract definition used to solve adjustment problems
d) a set of theories systematically integrated

_____ 13. A scale, constructed by scaling procedures,

a) varies from 0 to 3
b) has numerical properties
c) is a reliable measurement
d) is a valid measurement

_____ 14. Observational procedures

a) are based on interviews in general
b) are almost always highly systematic
c) frequently involve the informal recording
of observed behavior

d) almost never involve descriptions designed to test particular hypotheses

_____ 15. Experiments

a) involve actively changing a situation
b) are illustrated by the study of the aged in Chapter 6
c) focus on a situation at one point in time
d) rarely involve control procedures

_____ 16. Control procedures

a) enable investigators to deal effectively with research assistants
b) enable researchers to manage respondents effectively
c) prevent outside factors from interfering with the hypotheses being tested
d) enable researchers to develop operational definitions

_____ 17. "Difference is significant at the .01 level" means that

a) the results are highly important and might well be the basis for further investigations
b) results are trivial or unimportant
c) there are 99 chances out of 100 that the sample result would not also be true for the population
d) there is 1 chance out of 100 that the sample result would not also be true for the population

_____ 18. If results from the study of older people were true for people in general, then we would expect that

a) older people who see themselves as old would tend to be maladjusted in comparison to those who see themselves as middle-aged
b) older widows and widowers would tend to be adjusted in comparison to older people who are married and living with their spouses
c) older people who see themselves as middle-aged would tend to be maladjusted in comparison to those who see themselves as old
d) older employed individuals would tend to

be maladjusted in comparison to older retired individuals

_____ 19. The conclusion, from the study of older people
in Chapter 6, that compulsory retirement is
the major cause of maladjustment in American
society

a) is not warranted by the evidence presented
b) is a causal oversimplification
c) both of the above
d) neither of the above

_____ 20. With respect to the study of older people in
Chapter 6, structural-functional orientation
might suggest that

a) work must have important functions for
society if maladjustment is associated
with retirement
b) there is a conflict between society's role
for the aged and the self-image of many
older individuals
c) it is vital to determine the net balance of
positive and negative reinforcers within
any given role loss or role gain
d) our commonsense theories about the effects
of retirement generally function incorrectly

Concept Recognition: Write the concept or term in the
blank space next to its definition.

_____ 1. A procedure for collecting information through actively changing a situation and
systematically recording results obtained under two
or more conditions.

_____ 2. The study of the relationship
between the knowledge people collect and the social
structures surrounding these efforts.

_____ 3. An unprejudiced orientation or
openness to information about the true nature of
reality.

_____ 4. Correspondence between the
measurement and the variable it is designed to
measure.

_____ 5. The use of multiple theories

or methods of investigation.

_____ 6. A concept which divides phenomena into two or more categories.

_____ 7. The measurement's lack of variation over time (stability) and consistency when
used at the same time in different situations (equivalence).

_____ 8. Procedures for measuring the
phenomena a concept refers to.

_____ 9. Techniques for selecting the
"sample" or the units to be observed, usually individuals, from the larger population being investigated.

_____10. A measurement with numerical
properties.

True/False: Enter "T" for true or "F" for false for the
best answer to the statement.

_____ 1. C. Wright Mills was the founder of the sociology
of knowledge.

_____ 2. Research triangulation requires the use of all
known theories and all known data-collection
procedures.

_____ 3. Ad hominem is the technique of attacking or
defending a theory through an evaluation of
those who put the theory forward.

_____ 4. The fallacy of division is reasoning that what
is true for the whole is also true for every
part.

_____ 5. The definition of a research problem includes
outlining the general procedures to be used
for collecting evidence.

_____ 6. An independent variable in one study can be
a dependent variable in another study.

_____ 7. A probability sample cannot be used for the
purpose of drawing conclusions about the population from which the sample was drawn.

_____ 8. A highly reliable measurement is necessarily

quite valid.

_____ 9. A scale is a measurement which necessarily has numerical properties.

_____10. Control procedures are techniques which can be used within experiments.

Concept Definition: Write the definition of the concept or term appearing on the left in the blank space next to it.

1. precision of measurement _____

_____

2. control procedures _____

_____

3. dependent variable _____

_____

4. evidence _____

_____

5. interview survey _____

_____

6. probability sample _____

_____

7. questionnaire survey _____

_____

8. independent variable _____

_____

9. bias _____

_____

10. observation _____

_____

ANSWERS

Self Quiz

1.	d	6.	a	11.	c	16.	c
2.	d	7.	c	12.	a	17.	d
3.	d	8.	c	13.	b	18.	a
4.	a	9.	b	14.	c	19.	c
5.	b	10.	a	15.	a	20.	a

Concept Recognition

1. experiment
2. sociology of knowledge
3. objectivity
4. validity of measurement
5. research triangulation

6. variable
7. reliability of measurement
8. operational definition
9. sampling procedures
10. scale

True-False

1.	F	6.	T
2.	F	7.	F
3.	T	8.	F
4.	T	9.	T
5.	T	10.	T

Concept Definition

See Glossary in back of this booklet

Introduction to Social Stratification

7

OVERVIEW

Stratification, or the structuring of social inequality, has changed from a two-class system with a
tiny class at the top in preindustrial society to (for
Weber) multiple categories with stratification along
the separate dimensions of income or wealth, status and
power. For Marx, however, industrial society is characterized by conflict between owners (bourgeoisie) and
workers (proletariat), and class warfare is necessary
if the workers are to produce a genuinely equalitarian
society. Contrary to the equalitarian ideals of American society, structured inequalities do exist here as
well as in other societies. For example, they occur
with respect to income, occupational status, power and
education.

7.1 The Nature of Stratification

a Social Mobility

Social stratification refers to the structuring or
persistence of social categories or groupings that
tend to maintain social inequality. Thus, a strat-
ified society is one in which extremely rapid social
mobility--or movement up or down society's various
ladders (such as income and occupational status or

prestige)--does not occur. Shaw's Pygmalion illustrates a situation in which upward mobility within
a stratification system does in fact occur. Eliza
Doolittle, a flower girl, moves up largely on the
basis of changes in speech patterns and the learning of etiquette. The long-term trend in societies
has been toward increasing upward social mobility.
This is illustrated by the decline of the caste
system in India, where no (or almost no) mobility
from one caste to another was possible. It is also
illustrated by changes within preindustrial societies
generally: from two-class systems with a tiny elite
at the top to three-class systems with a relatively
large middle class. The middle class includes professionals, managers, shopkeepers, office workers
and salespeople. And the vast peasantry gives way
both to middle-class occupations as well as to
skilled, semi-skilled and unskilled manual work.

b Class, Status and Power

Marx viewed a class as including people in a similar
relationship to the means of production, such as
workers as distinct from owners. For Marx, a class
necessarily develops class consciousness (awareness
of their class membership and necessarily moves on
to take part in a class struggle. He believed that,
at some time in the future, such struggles would
result in a classless or equalitarian society.
Weber, by constrast, did not see a class as necessarily developing class consciousness or taking
political action within a class struggle. He emphasized three different dimensions of social stratification: wealth or income (the criterion for
distinguishing among the social classes), status
or prestige, and power. Thus, people can be high
on some dimensions of stratification and low on
others (status inconsistency), and a class struggle
is not inevitable. American sociologists generally
accept Weber's approach more than Marx's. For example, Warner's study of a New England town distinguishes between a class made up of newly-rich
people and a class with old wealth and, therefore,
higher status. There is another concept of equality
sociologists use distinct from classless or equalitarian society. It is equality of opportunity, referring to similar chances to attain high positions
in the stratification system.

7.2 Stratification in Industrial Society

a Changes in Occupational Structure

A fundamental alteration in industrial economies, one with important implications for social stratification, is the shift from the farm to the factory and white collar world. In the U.S., for example, the number of farms and proportion of the labor force engaged in farming have dramatically decreased while the average size of farms has greatly increased. Along with such changes have come increases in the proportion of workers classified as professional and technical, managerial, sales, and white collar generally. These changes are only recently occurring among nonwhites.

b Structured Inequalities in the United States

Associated with changes in occupational structure are changes in social stratification. Although the long-term trend in the U.S. has been toward increasing opportunities for upward mobility, there is some conflicting short term evidence with regard to the "inheritance" of occupations (or lack of mobility from one generation to the next). A study in Indianapolis indicates an increase in such inheritance. As for the distribution of poverty and wealth, studies indicate a continuing decline in the percentage of people below the poverty level, and this is paralleled by indicators of economic well-being other than income. College attendance by high school graduates is closely tied to family income, and such attendance in turn tends to be closely related to the lifetime income of these students. Thus, granting that education is perhaps the major ladder up the stratification system for most individuals, it also works to perpetuate inequalities. Sometimes this process is complex. For example, the children of managers may be taught verbal skills; and those managers in turn may influence school systems to give much greater encouragement to children with such skills. This illustrates the dimension of power as well as education. In another study focusing on power, income and education were found to be more closely related among employers than among managers, and even less closely related among workers. Thus, education tends to have a greater economic "pay off" the higher one rises occupationally.

c   Structured Inequalities in Other Countries

Social stratification, or the existence of structured inequalities, exists throughout the world,
despite political ideologies to the contrary. However, it appears that gaps between the rich and
the poor are not generally as great in the socialist societies of Eastern Europe as in Western
Europe or the U.S. According to one study, both
a long history of experience with political democracy and especially a history of strong socialist
movements are associated with the equalitarian
redistribution of income. However, these latter
movements tend to be associated with less higher
education on the part of working class youth, perhaps due to a lesser emphasis on achievement. In
China, there is an arrangement known as "taking
the backdoor," which refers to the trading of favors
in violation of strict standards of equality.

d   The Hidden Injuries of Class Membership

The "injuries" to individuals at a given level
within a stratification system are not always obvious or material. For example, Carl Dorrian, a
young electrician apprentice, likes his work and
makes a good income, but he is not really content.
He feels that he has no personal control over his
work situation, that he's held back because he's
working for someone. And Carl, a pipe fitter who
makes double the salary of the middle-aged schoolteacher who is his next door neighbor, nevertheless
calls that teacher "Mister" and is in turn called
by his first name. In addition to such hidden injuries, we should not forget the more obvious injuries. For example, a schoolteacher is generally
higher than a skilled worker in prestige, but his
income may be substantially lower. And in a society
in which inflation is continuing, public employees
like schoolteachers may have increasing difficulty
keeping up with the cost of living. In this situation, then, both the pipe fitter and the schoolteacher suffer, but from different kinds of injuries.

SELF-QUIZ

Multiple Choice: In the space provided, enter the letter
of the answer that best completes the question.

_____ 1. A system of social stratification

   a) does not exist in an equalitarian society
   b) does not exist in a classless society
   c) both of the above
   d) neither (a) nor (b)

_____ 2. Shaw's Pygmalion best illustrates

   a) upward mobility
   b) horizontal mobility
   c) downward mobility
   d) intergenerational mobility

_____ 3. In a caste system

   a) upward mobility is more prevalent than down-
      ward mobility
   b) downward mobility is more prevalent than
      upward mobility
   c) caste membership is determined on the basis
      of school performance
   d) caste membership is determined at birth

_____ 4. Preindustrial societies in general are char-
         acterized by

   a) the existence of three classes
   b) the existence of a small elite, a large
      middle class, a moderately-large working
      class, and a large peasantry
   c) the existence of a small elite and a large
      peasantry
   d) high social mobility

_____ 5. In preindustrial China, as documented in a
         study by Hsu,

   a) a caste system existed
   b) a system of competitive examinations existed
   c) there was no significant upward mobility
   d) there was no significant horizontal mobility

_____ 6. With respect to a tie between class membership
         and class consciousness,

a) both Weber and Marx believed it to be inevitable
b) Marx but not Weber believed it to be inevitable
c) Weber but not Marx believed it to be inevitable
d) neither believed it to be inevitable

_____ 7. With respect to a tie between class member-
         ship and class political action,

a) both Weber and Marx believed it to be inevitable
b) Marx but not Weber believed it to be inevitable
c) Weber but not Marx believed it to be inevitable
d) neither believed it to be inevitable

_____ 8. According to Weber,

a) people in a given class will automatically
   behave as a status group
b) people in the same economic situation will
   automatically behave as a status group
c) people with a certain amount of class consciousness will automatically behave as
   a status group
d) none of the above

_____ 9. The existence of "status inconsistency" (with-
         out using this term) is emphasized by

a) Marx
b) Weber
c) both Marx and Weber
d) neither Marx nor Weber

_____ 10. Equality of opportunity refers to

a) equal or similar opportunities to attain
   high positions in the stratification system
b) the existence of a classless society
c) the existence of an equalitarian society
d) the existence of a society without social
   stratification

_____ 11. In the U.S. the occupational structure shifted
          so that

a) there is a substantial recent increase in the proportion of the labor force engaged in farming
b) the proportion of blue-collar workers has increased between 1960 and 1976
c) the proportion of white-collar workers has increased between 1960 and 1976
d) the proportion of private household workers has increased between 1960 and 1976

_____ 12. Between 1960 and 1976 in the U.S.

a) the percent of nonwhites working on farms has increased
b) the percent of nonwhites working as non-farm laborers has increased
c) the percent of nonwhites working as private household workers has increased
d) the percent of nonwhites who are white-collar workers has increased

_____ 13. Intergenerational mobility, based on an Indianapolis study, is

a) decreasing
b) remaining about the same
c) increasing slightly
d) increasing rapidly

_____ 14. The percent of people in the U.S. below the poverty level, in the period between 1959 and 1976, has

a) been approximately cut in half
b) decreased slightly
c) remained about the same
d) increased

_____ 15. With respect to the presence of possessions in the U.S. homes in 1976,

a) three-quarters or more had at least one car
b) one-quarter or less had one car
c) half or less had a television set
d) half or less had a telephone

_____ 16. In the U.S., with regard to the relationship between educational level and lifetime income,

a) college graduates make no more than high-school graduates

81

b) high-school graduates make no more than
   elementary-school graduates
c) college graduates make over twice as much
   as elementary-school graduates
d) college graduates make no more than elementary-school graduates

_____ 17. For high-school graduates whose family earned
        $15,000 or more, the chances that they were
        attending college in 1967 was

        a) about six times as great as for those whose
           family earned under $3,000
        b) about twice as great as for those whose
           family earned under $3,000
        c) about 1 1/2 times as great as for those
           whose family earned under $3,000
        d) about 1 1/4 times as great as for those
           whose family earned under $3,000

_____ 18. According to a study comparing employers, man-
        agers and workers, income and education were

        a) more closely related for workers than for
           managers
        b) more closely related for managers than for
           employers
        c) more closely related for workers than for
           employers
        d) more closely related for employers than for
           managers

_____ 19. With respect to the economic gap between the
        rich and the poor,

        a) it tends to be greater in the Soviet Union
           than the U.S.
        b) it tends to be about the same in the U.S.
           as in the socialist societies of Eastern
           Europe
        c) it tends to be less in the socialist soci-
           eties of Eastern Europe than in the U.S.
        d) none of the above

_____ 20. The "hidden injuries" of class membership refer
        to

        a) income disadvantages
        b) age disadvantages
        c) wealth disadvantages
        d) nonmaterial disadvantages

Concept Recognition: Write the concept or term in the blank space next to its definition.

_____ 1. A social category with its members in the same economic situation.

_____ 2. Degree of honor or prestige given by or received from society.

_____ 3. A hierarchy (from high to low) of social categories which structures social in-equality.

_____ 4. Differences between the individ-ual's positions on several planes or dimensions of stratification.

_____ 5. Mobility within the lifetime of the individual.

_____ 6. The movement of individuals from lower to higher or higher to lower social cat-egories in a social stratification system.

_____ 7. A social category whose members have a similar relationship to the means of produc-tion and who, at some point, develop class conscious-ness.

_____ 8. A social stratification system in which no (or almost no) mobility from one social category to another is possible.

_____ 9. People's differences in the attainment or possession of whatever society values.

_____10. A situation in which all mem-bers of society have equal or similar opportunities to attain positions on the higher levels of the stratification system.

True/False: Enter "T" for true or "F" for false for the best answer to the statement.

_____ 1. Social stratification exists in the Soviet Union.

_____ 2. In industrial society, the long-range trend has been a decrease in the prevalence of up-ward social mobility.

_____ 3. Contemporary industrial societies generally have caste systems.

_____ 4. Warner found the newly-rich people in "Yankee City" to be in the same status group as those with old wealth.

_____ 5. If there is equality of opportunity in society, then a classless society exists.

_____ 6. If there is equality of opportunity in society, then an equalitarian society exists.

_____ 7. Little is known about intragenerational mobility in comparison to intergenerational mobility.

_____ 8. In 1972 the wealthiest one percent of the U.S. population owned over twenty percent of the nation's wealth.

_____ 9. The variable of education in the U.S. is closely related to lifetime income.

_____10. It is no longer possible to compare bourgeoisie and proletariat attitudes in contemporary questionnaire surveys.

Concept Definition: Write the definition of the concept or term appearing on the left in the blank space next to it.

1. class system _____

_____

2. class consciousness _____

_____

3. class (based on Marx) _____

_____

4. caste _____

_____

5. exploitation of others _____

_____

6. class (based on Weber) _____

_____

7. equalitarian society _____

_____

8. intergenerational mobility _____

_____

9. classless society _____

_____

10. social equality _____

_____

ANSWERS

Self Quiz

1.	c	6.	b	11.	c	16.	c
2.	a	7.	b	12.	d	17.	a
3.	d	8.	d	13.	a	18.	d
4.	c	9.	b	14.	a	19.	c
5.	b	10.	a	15.	a	20.	d

Concept Recognition

1. class
2. status
3. social stratification
4. status inconsistency
5. intragenerational mobility
6. social mobility
7. class
8. caste system
9. social inequality
10. equality of opportunity

True-False

1.	T	6.	F
2.	F	7.	T
3.	F	8.	T
4.	F	9.	T
5.	F	10.	F

Concept Definition

See Glossary in back of this booklet

Ethnic Groups

8

OVERVIEW

Ethnic groups, based on ancestry (race, religion, national origin), exist in an ethnic stratification system with a given country. Members of a given ethnic group--as portrayed by Ralph Ellison, a black writer-- are often treated as "invisible" with respect to unique or individual human characteristics by others. However, in addition to such prejudice and discrimination we can view each ethnic group on its own terms, with its members using ethnic relationships as a way of achieving community or gemeinschaft. This search for ethnic identity is producing a trend toward cultural pluralism in American society as distinct from an earlier push toward amalgamation or assimilation (in which ethnic differences would be greatly reduced).

SYNOPSIS

8.1 What Are Ethnic Groups?

   a Ethnic Groups and Ethnicity

   Ethnic groups are people with a common ancestry who either see themselves as belonging to a common cat- egory or are seen in that way by others. As Ellison portrays, that category can become so important to others that the ethnic, as a unique individual, becomes invisible. In addition to seeing ethnic groups in this all-or-none way, we can also view ethnicity as a matter of the degree of identification (by self or others) with an ethnic group.

b   Ethnic Differences

Are there genuine differences between different ethnic groups? Are differences no more than the product of prejudice? In a study by Greeley and McCready, American males of Italian and Anglo-Saxon origin were compared, and a number of differences were found despite the changes from one generation to the next: differences with respect to fatalism, political campaigning activities, membership in civic organization, and so on. Of course, such differences are no more than tendencies within each ethnic group, and any given individual can easily differ from such tendencies. These differences were related to differences between Italian and Anglo-Saxon culture. For example, Italian fatalism is related to the influences of the Catholic Church as well as to the collapsing social structure in southern Italy at the time of heavy emigration to the U.S. Given that ethnic differences do exist, it is useful to learn about the nature of such differences in order to begin to understand people having a different ethnic background from our own, provided that we make no assumption that every member of the ethnic group conforms to the general pattern.

8.2   Ethnic Stratification

a   From Paternalistic to Competitive Race Relations

An ethnic stratification system is a particular kind of social stratification system, one in which the individual is assigned to his or her social category at birth. Thus, an ethnic stratification system is a caste system. Paternalistic race relations, characteristic of many preindustrial societies, tend to involve relationships in which the dominant group gives little responsibility to the subservient group and provides for that group's basic needs. It is illustrated by the relationship between black slave and white master in the American South prior to the Civil War. Race relations tend to be relatively stable, and although the subordinate group is by no means happy with the situation, there tends to be little active plotting of rebellion. Competitive race relations are characteristic of industrial societies. In such societies, different ethnic groups are rivals for scarce resources. The slave or servant gives way to the employee and the master is replaced by the employer. Here, there tends to be sharp increases and decreases in prejudice, as distinct from a relatively stable situation.

b   Racial Inequalities in Contemporary American Society

In the U.S. there are definite and persistent inequalities between blacks and whites with respect to employment in higher-status occupations as well as income. For example, in 1960 only 16.1 percent of nonwhites were white-collar workers, compared to 46.6 percent of whites. However, between 1960 and 1976 the difference between these two ethnic groups was greatly reduced: nonwhites increased to 34.7 percent (more than doubling their percentage) and whites increased to 51.8 percent. Yet during this same period, unemployment rates for nonwhites have persisted at approximately double that for whites. And during this period, income differences between whites and nonwhites were maintained, although the income of both groups has increased.

c   Davies' Theory of Revolution

One aspect of industrial society is a revolution of rising expectations, or a continuing rise in people's aspirations. Davies, a political scientist, has related such rises to revolutions. He finds that when rising aspirations (or expected need satisfactions) are not accompanied by actual need satisfactions, an intolerable gap between what people want and what they get is created. The result is revolution or revolt, or the basis for violence. This can be illustrated by the urban riots in the U.S. during the late 1960s. The typical black rioter was someone whose aspirations had been rising, such as someone better educated than his or her black neighbors, yet almost invariably employed in a menial job or underemployed. On a societal scale, blacks came to expect rapid changes in education as a result of the 1954 Brown decision of the U.S. Supreme Court. But integration proceded very slowly, with much of it on a token basis. And segregation in many Northern cities has been growing, largely because of shifts in residential patterns, such as the departure of many whites from cities to suburbs.

d Prejudice and Discrimination

Prejudice refers to negative beliefs and feelings against ethnic group members, whereas discrimination refers to actions that create disadvantages for such individuals. A white employer may, for example, maintain his or her prejudice while still hiring a black person. In a study of prejudice against Puerto Ricans, Levin found that relative evaluators--people who tend to compare their performance with that of others--tended to increase their prejudice against Puerto Ricans when they were frustrated. Self evaluators, who tend to assess themselves in comparison to their own previous performances, did not tend to increase their prejudice under the same conditions. Studies of relative deprivation--a concept combining relative evaluation and frustration--in the U.S. army during World War II show that it is linked to morale. Relative deprivation appears to be structured in society by the social stratification system.

e The Intelligence Controversy

Arthur Jensen and Richard Herrnstein have precipitated considerable controversy with their statements that black children with lower IQ scores than white children indicates an inherent racial inferiority. However, Jensen has considerably altered his earlier view, based on his more recent work, and he now sees environmental factors as playing a dominant role in such differences in IQ. Many other social scientists have brought forward research and interpretations which lead to the general conclusion that no proof of genetic inequality in intelligence between blacks and whites exists. Several studies severely criticize IQ scores as measures of mental capacity.

8.3 Cultural Pluralism

a Amalgamation, Assimilation and Cultural Pluralism

A focus on ethnic stratification provides only one dimension for understanding the situation of a given ethnic group, namely, its relationships with

89

other groups. But another important dimension has
to do with internal events within the ethnic group:
where does it wish to go, and where is it going?
Within American society, one of our most cherished
ideals has been the idea of the melting pot: the
notion that the various ethnic groups coming to our
shores would become assimilated. That is, they
would submerge their unique ethnic characteristics
and all become similar: Americans. Recently, the
ideal of cultural pluralism, which does not involve
such submergence yet nevertheless includes a certain degree of contact with other groups, has been
emphasized. It involves more contact than segregation but less than assimilation or amalgamation.

b   Ethnicity as a Search for Gemeinschaft

According to Greeley, the search for ethnic identity
implied within cultural pluralism illustrates the
more general search for gemeinschaft, or community.
We live in an urbanized, bureaucratized society,
says Greeley, in which many of our social relationships are transitory or superficial. An emphasis
on ethnic background can help provide the individual
with close relationships, and thus provide some
balance in his or her life.

SELF-QUIZ

Multiple Choice: In the space provided, enter the letter of the answer that best completes the question.

_____ 1. Ethnicity

   a) is a variable which can take on more than two different degrees
   b) is a variable which is of the "either-or" type
   c) is not a variable
   d) none of the above

_____ 2. Which of these differences, based on a study by Greeley and McCready, is incorrect for males:

   a) Italian-Americans tend to be more fatalistic than Anglo-Saxons
   b) Italian-Americans tend to be more sexually permissive in their attitudes
   c) Italian-Americans tend to be less active in political campaigns
   d) Italian-Americans tend to join fewer civic organizations

_____ 3. Differences in attitudes toward fatalism between Italian-American males and males of Anglo-Saxon origin

   a) are not related to differences between Italian and Anglo-Saxon culture
   b) are not related to differences between Catholicism and Protestantism
   c) are related to the collapsing social structure in southern Italy 50 to 100 years ago
   d) are related to the relationship between Protestants and Catholics in Italy

_____ 4. An ethnic stratification system is

   a) not a caste system
   b) not a social stratification system
   c) not based on the assignment of individuals to strata as a result of their achievement
   d) not the result of placing individuals in social categories at birth

_____ 5. Competitive race relations

   a) is characteristic of preindustrial society
   b) is characterized by relative stable rela-
      tionships
   c) is characterized by powerlessness of the
      oppressed group
   d) is characteristic of industrial society

_____ 6. Inequalities between whites and nonwhites in
American society with regard to employment

   a) are rapidly decreasing with regard to per-
      cent employed in white-collar work
   b) are being maintained with regard to percent
      employed in white-collar work
   c) are rapidly decreasing with regard to un-
      employment rates
   d) are decreasing at a moderate rate with
      regard to unemployment rates

_____ 7. Inequalities between whites and nonwhites in
American society with regard to income

   a) are rapidly decreasing
   b) are being maintained at about the same level
   c) are increasing slowly
   d) are increasing rapidly

_____ 8. Davies' theory of revolution

   a) differs markedly from Crane Brinton's
      approach in his Anatomy of Revolution
   b) disputes the importance of the so-called
      revolution of rising expectations
   c) can be stated verbally but cannot be graphed
   d) centers on the gap between what people want
      and what they get

_____ 9. According to Davies' theory of revolution, in
order to stop a revolution,

   a) raise aspirations
   b) raise expectations
   c) lower need satisfactions
   d) raise need satisfactions, but raise aspira-
      tions much higher than need satisfactions

_____ 10. Davies' theory of revolution can be applied to

a) violent societal revolutions
b) internal violent revolts, such as urban riots
c) both of the above
d) neither a) nor b)

_____ 11. Prejudice and discrimination are related in that

a) discrimination refers to actions, not prejudice
b) prejudice refers to actions, not discrimination
c) both refer to actions
d) both refer to beliefs and feelings

_____ 12. Relative evaluators tend to be more prejudiced when frustrated than self evaluators because

a) they generally hate other people
b) they have more to gain personally by putting others down
c) frustration upsets them more
d) they are more oriented to prejudice

_____ 13. Interest in which of these indicates self evaluation:

a) Mary's algebra grade was higher than the class average
b) Mary's algebra grade was lower than her best friend's grade
c) Mary's algebra grade was lower than her last year's grade in mathematics
d) Mary's algebra grade was lower than the class average

_____ 14. Reference groups and relative deprivation are related in that

a) both are based on self evaluation
b) both are based on relative evaluation
c) both imply frustration on the part of the individual
d) both apply primarily to the army situation

_____ 15. Social stratification and relative deprivation are related in that

a) social stratification tends to structure

relative deprivation
b) both build scarcity into society
c) both provide one basis for prejudice in society
d) all of the above

_____ 16. Al Capp's Kigmies get rid of prejudice and discrimination in society because

a) they serve as scapegoats
b) they kick others around
c) they understand the causes of prejudice and discrimination
d) they convince others to change their stereotypes

_____ 17. Evidence on the relation between mental capacity and race (blacks and whites) indicates

a) proof of genetic inequality
b) proof of genetic equality
c) strong evidence for genetic inequality
d) none of the above

_____ 18. Kagan's analysis of the relationship between IQ and basic mental capacity indicates that

a) it is unreasonal to assume that the Wechsler Test has anything to do with basic mental capacity
b) the Wechsler test is an excellent measure of basic mental capacity
c) the Wechsler test is a fair measure of basic mental capacity
d) the Wechsler test is barely adequate as a measure of basic mental capacity

_____ 19. Which of these involves the greatest degree of cultural contact:

a) cultural pluralism
b) assimilation
c) segregation
d) amalgamation

_____ 20. Ethnicity, gemeinschaft and gessellschaft are related in that (according to Greeley)

a) none of them is present in industrial society
b) ethnicity is a means to achieving gesellschaft

94

c) ethnicity is a means of achieving <u>gemeinschaft</u>
d) <u>gemeinschaft</u> and <u>gesellschaft</u> are rough synonyms

Concept Recognition: Write the concept or term in the blank space next to its definition.

_____ 1. Negative beliefs or expectations and feelings directed against members of an ethnic group.

_____ 2. The process by which an ethnic culture is altered in important respects so as to conform to a dominant culture.

_____ 3. Relationships in which one group is subservient to another, given little responsibility and has basic needs provided for.

_____ 4. A pattern of ethnic group relations in which each ethnic group retains its fundamental values and norms yet incorporates certain elements from the others.

_____ 5. The mixing of cultures (and sometimes races as well) to form a new culture (and sometimes a new racial type).

_____ 6. A feeling of unjustified loss or frustration relative to others.

_____ 7. Actions creating disadvantages for members of an ethnic group compared to others.

_____ 8. A set of individuals who see themselves or are seen by others as belonging to a certain social category because of their common ancestry.

_____ 9. A hierarchy of ethnic groups which structures social inequality.

_____10. Degree of identification by self or others with an ethnic group.

True/False: Enter "T" for true or "F" for false for the best answer to the statement.

_____ 1. European immigrant IQ scores during the 1920s were almost identical to black scores today.

_____ 2. The melting pot ideal is similar to an emphasis
          on the importance of cultural pluralism.

_____ 3. Differences between Italian-Americans and Anglo-
          Saxons are not statistically significant.

_____ 4. According to Davies, revolutions occur during
          a period of rising aspirations or expected
          need satisfactions.

_____ 5. Self evaluators tend to compare their perfor-
          mances with those of others

_____ 6. A reference group is any group whatsoever that
          provides a basis for evaluating behavior.

_____ 7. Relative deprivation includes the ideas of
          frustration and relative evaluation.

_____ 8. Arthur Jensen has modified his earlier state-
          ments to emphasize the role of environment in
          affecting the IQ of black children.

_____ 9. There is some relationship between an ethnic
          group's position in the ethnic stratification
          system and its average IQ.

_____10. In reviewing Myrdal's An American Dilemma,
          Ralph Ellison said that there is more to the
          problems faced by blacks than their relations
          with whites.

Concept Definition: Write the definition of the concept
or term appearing on the left in the blank space next to
it.

1. self evaluators _____

_____

2. scapegoat _____

_____

3. revolution of rising expectations _____

_____

4. cultural contact _____

_____

96

5. strata _____

_____

6. ethnicity _____

_____

7. relative evaluators _____

_____

8. relative deprivation _____

_____

9. competitive relationships _____

_____

10. reference group _____

_____

ANSWERS

Self Quiz

1.	a	6.	a	11.	a	16.	a
2.	b	7.	b	12.	b	17.	d
3.	c	8.	d	13.	c	18.	a
4.	c	9.	d	14.	b	19.	d
5.	d	10.	b	15.	d	20.	c

Concept Recognition

1. prejudice
2. assimilation
3. paternalistic relationships
4. cultural pluralism
5. amalgamation
6. relative deprivation
7. discrimination
8. ethnic group
9. ethnic stratifica-
    tion
10. ethnicity

True-False

1.	T	6.	T
2.	F	7.	T
3.	F	8.	T
4.	T	9.	T
5.	F	10.	T

Concept Definition

See Glossary in back of this booklet

Sex and Age Roles
9

OVERVIEW

   Sex stratification, although based on biological
gender, is largely a product of social roles constructed
by societies. In industrial societies it appears that
a double stratification system is produced: men tend
to be on top with respect to income, occupational status
and education, and women tend to be on top with respect
to power in one-to-one personal situations with men
(as depicted in Ibsen's A Doll's House). Age stratification is based on chronological age, but it too is very
much a role phenomenon. Sex and age role pluralism provide an alternative direction to that of rigid stratification systems.

SYNOPSIS

9.1 Sex Roles

   a Sex Stratification

      Gender refers to inherited biological character-
      istics, whereas a sex role--associated with a
      given gender--is a social role constructed by
      society. That role can vary greatly from one
      society to another, as illustrated by Mead's study
      of peoples of New Guinea: Arapesh men and women
      are maternal and responsive; Mundugumor men and

99

women are both aggressive and ruthless; and Tchambuli women are dominant over their men. In industrial societies, sex roles are influenced by biological differences but are not biologically determined.

Sexism refers to prejudice or discrimination against members of a given gender, and such behavior is also constructed by society. Despite the women's liberation movement, income differences between men and women increased between 1959 and 1974, although black women did not do as badly as white women. Discrimination in promotions is illustrated by the small percentage of women achieving the rank of full professor in one university. Prejudice is less tangible than discrimination and therefore more difficult to document. It is illustrated by the language people use. For example, angry men may be called outraged whereas angry women may be called hysterical, illustrating sexism against women. Sexism against men is illustrated by calling thoughtful women considerate and thoughtful men over-sensitive. Nora's rejection of Helmer's sexual advances in Ibsen's A Doll's House may stem in part from sexist attitudes associated with Victorian roles for men and women. There, the sexual interests of males are suspect, being considered bestial in nature, whereas women are supposed to exhibit no such interests. The "Ten Commandments of Masculinity" further illustrate sexism against men: they should not display fear or express themselves emotionally, but they should always be logical, specialize in their jobs, and have the answer to all questions at all times.

b   Sex Role Pluralism

Sex role pluralism is an example of cultural pluralism (Chapter 8), and it is further illustrated by the process of role accumulation. There, the individual expands his or her set of roles or expands any given role to include elements of other roles. Thus, a woman might expand her feminine role to include intellectual elements from the masculine role. In sex role pluralism, each sex role retains its own fundamental values and norms while incorporating such elements from the other.

Comics, fiction and news stories may be used to illustrate sex role pluralism. Supergirl is

beautiful and she is also very brainy and tremen-
dously strong. Lady Sif is beautiful, sympathetic
and yearns to be close to Thor. Also, she is very
brave and an excellent fighter. Supermen, who used
to fly away from Lois Lane after saving her, now
stops long enough to kiss her. Nancy Drew is daring
and competent as well as pretty, differing from the
nuturant heroines of the "nurse" books. And in the
newspapers we find stories such as one about rapid
increases in the number of women criminals, illustrating the new careers opening up to women. Stories
about increased rights for gays and prostitutes
suggest that sex roles are being expanded so as to
include behavior formerly forbidden.

c Sex Roles and Cultural Change

Changes in sex roles indicate fundamental shifts in
culture and society. A scientific paradigm is a
system of assumptions (both explicit and implicit)
on which a science is based, such as the view of
space and time as absolutes within Newtonian physics,
Einstein put forward a contrasting paradigm, in
which time and space are relative to one another.
Similarly, we can speak of absolutist and relativistic cultural paradigms. A cultural paradigm is
a system of assumptions (both explicit and implicit) on which a culture is based. Victorian
morality, with its absolute views as to exactly
what is right and wrong in every aspect of sexual
behavior, is part of a cultural paradigm stressing
moral absolutism in all aspects of behavior. By
contrast, current rejections of Victorian morality
appear to be moving in a relativistic direction.
Premarital intercourse, homosexuality and even the
enjoyment of sex for its own sake are coming to be
evaluated only in relation to, or relative to, the
overall human situation within which they occur.
A procedure which may be involved in achieving a
shift in cultural paradigm is that of bracketing,
in which belief in existing assumptions is sus-
pended. Such a difficult process is aided by
greater awareness of the nature of one's existing
assumptions.

9.2 Age Roles

a Age Stratification

Age roles can be distinguished from chronological

age just as sex roles can be distinguished from gender. Whereas chronological age refers to age in years (referring to physical time), an age role is a social role (socially constructed) associated with a given chronological age.

Age stratification, in which inequalities are structured on the basis of chronological age, exists alongside of sex stratification in industrial societies. It is illustrated by the forcible retirement of individuals after they reach a certain chronological age regardless of their health. This produces age role discontinuity, or sharply altered age roles with advancing age. Such discontinuity contrasts with the continuity achieved by the Papago Indians of Arizona. This is illustrated by the three-year-old gradually learning to take on new responsibilities, such as shutting a heavy door. Age role discontinuities appear to be severe for women in American society even when retirement is not an issue. Standards for female beauty require youth far more than standards for male beauty (a double standard), and the change in the way an older woman's looks are evaluated by others may devastate her.

Ageism, or prejudice or discrimination against members of a given age category, is analogous to sexism. The role of the aged in American society includes many sexist ideas, such as the expectation that old people need not or should not lead an active sex life. Myths about older individuals, such as that they are generally sick and rigid persist in part because of the pressures of an age stratification system which keeps them at the bottom and a culture which values youth. Gray power refers to political efforts by older people to act in their own interests, such as the elimination of compulsory retirement.

b   Alternative Perspectives on the Roles of Older People

Disengagement theory and activity theory sharply differ in their approaches to the role of older people. Disengagement theory stresses the idea that death is inevitable and, therefore, the individual should begin to prepare for it by gradually withdrawing from relationships with others. Activity theory emphasizes the importance for the older person of continuing his or her patterns of activity and social involvement, with maladjustment seen as resulting from decreased activities and involvement.

Age role pluralism is analogous both to sex role pluralism and to cultural pluralism. Each age role retains its fundamental values and norms and also comes to include elements from the others. Thus, one individual might take on new activities--such as political involvement--whereas another might not. Age role pluralism is illustrated by the film Harold and Maude, depicting the development of an intimate relationship between a teen-age boy and an 80-year-old woman. Maude believes that her nearness to death does not require her to adopt a death-like social role, and she expresses herself both by taking time to enjoy flowers and by being free to "reach out," "take a chance" and even "get hurt."

Multiple Choice: In the space provided, enter the letter of the answer that best completes the question.

_____ 1. Gender and sex role are related in that

    a) both are based almost completely on what society does
    b) both are based almost completely on human biology
    c) sex roles are social roles associated with a given gender
    d) gender is constructed by a given sex role

_____ 2. Within Tchambuli culture, as reported by Mead,

    a) women tend to dominate men
    b) men tend to dominate women
    c) both men and women are maternal in orientation
    d) both men and women are aggressive in orientation

_____ 3. Sex roles in most preindustrial societies

    a) have men responsible for cooking
    b) have women responsible for herding and fishing
    c) have men responsible for gathering herbs and fruits
    d) have men responsible for clearing the land for crops

_____ 4. U.S. sex differences in earnings between 1959 and 1974 indicate that

    a) the income gap between males and females decreased greatly
    b) the income gap between males and females decreased slightly
    c) the income gap between males and females remained about the same
    d) the income gap between males and females increased

_____ 5. An illustration of sexism against men is

    a) calling efficient men "competent" and efficient women "compulsive"

    b) calling thoughtful women "considerate" and thoughtful men "over-sensitive"
    c) calling industrious men "hard workers" and industrious women "drudges"
    d) calling ordinary-looking men "pleasant looking" and ordinary-looking women "homely"

_____ 6. The Victorian sex role for women

    a) gave middle-class women freedom to enjoy sexual relations
    b) was constructed partially around the fact that a large surplus of women was created in the labor market
    c) enabled middle-class women to sharply differentiate themselves from other women
    d) was a product of the late nineteenth century

_____ 7. Within Victorian sex roles,

    a) men's interest in sex is viewed as the product of a bestial nature
    b) men could use the power of guilt to achieve sexual ends
    c) the two-career family came to be important
    d) women were no longer exhibits of leisure for their husbands

_____ 8. The "Ten Commandments of Masculinity" do not include:

    a) Thou shalt be condescending to women
    b) Thus shalt not cry or display fear, weakness, sympathy, empathy
    c) Thou shalt listen for the sake of listening
    d) Thou shalt control thy wife's body

_____ 9. Role accumulation is illustrated by

    a) a man incorporating emotional elements of the feminine role into the masculine role
    b) an individual increasing the number of roles he or she plays
    c) both of the above
    d) neither of the above

_____ 10. Sex role pluralism is illustrated by

    a) the bravery and emotional expressiveness

of Charlie's Angels
b) the adoring expressions of Lady Sif
c) the beauty of Supergirl
d) the strength of Superman

_____ 11. The situation with respect to women and crime in the U.S. is that

   a) women still tend to get preferential treatment in the courts
   b) women's property crimes are decreasing
   c) women's violent crimes are decreasing
   d) women's rate of embezzlement is decreasing

_____ 12. Prostitutes, at their national convention,

   a) generally would like to leave their profession if they could
   b) generally express little pride in their work
   c) generally complained about "male licentiousness"
   d) generally agreed that jailing prostitutes only insures that they'll never get another job

_____ 13. Increased rights for gays and prostitutes best illustrates

   a) sexism
   b) cultural pluralism
   c) a paradigm
   d) sex role discontinuity

_____ 14. A cultural paradigm is best illustrated by

   a) Einstein's theory of relativity
   b) Newton's theory of mechanics
   c) moral absolutism in most aspects of society
   d) a critique of Victorian morality

_____ 15. Bracketing is

   a) the acceptance of a given role
   b) suspending belief in existing assumptions
   c) awareness of a cultural paradigm
   d) accepting a cultural paradigm

_____ 16. Age roles are

a) based primarily on mathematical and physical
   factors
b) based primarily on physiological factors
c) based primarily on societal factors
d) based primarily on personality factors

_____ 17. The role of the aged in industrial society

   a) generally illustrates downward mobility
   b) generally illustrates lateral mobility
   c) generally illustrates upward mobility
   d) generally illustrates bracketing

_____ 18. Age role continuity is best illustrated by

   a) mental disorders among the aged in industrial
      society
   b) the shift from athletic hero to business
      executive
   c) the shift from campus beauty queen to wife
   d) the three-year-old Papago girl learning
      to shut a heavy door

_____ 19. The double standard of aging in American so-
         ciety refers to

   a) the different standards for boys and men
   b) the different standards for girls and women
   c) different standards of beauty for men and
      women
   d) different standards of sexual behavior for
      men and women

_____ 20. Ageism refers to

   a) prejudice but not discrimination
   b) neither prejudice nor discrimination
   c) discrimination but not prejudice
   d) prejudice or discrimination

Concept Recognition: Write the concept or term in the
blank space next to its definition.

_____ 1. Prejudice or discrimination
against members of a given gender.

_____ 2. A pattern of sex role relations
where each sex role retains its fundamental values
and norms yet incorporates elements from the other.

_____ 3. A social role associated with a given chronological age.

_____ 4. Sharply altered age roles with advancing chronological age.

_____ 5. The inherited or biological characteristics distinguishing one sex role from another.

_____ 6. A pattern of sex role relations where each sex role retains its fundamental values and norms yet incorporates elements from the other.

_____ 7. The suspension of belief in existing assumptions.

_____ 8. A theory emphasizing an inevitable mutual withdrawal--arising gradually-- between the aging person and others.

_____ 9. Prejudice or discrimination against members of a given age category.

_____10. A system of explicit and implicit assumptions on which a science is based.

True/False: Enter "T" for true or "F" for false for the best answer to the statement.

_____ 1. Activity theory and disengagement theory come to virtually identical conclusions.

_____ 2, Age role pluralism is illustrated by the film, Harold and Maude.

_____ 3. Black women in the U.S. have increased (between 1959 and 1974) their earnings as a percent of the earnings of black men.

_____ 4. A Doll's House illustrates sexism against men as well as against women.

_____ 5. The Victorian role for women is based in part on St. Paul's stress on the virtues of suppressing sexual feelings.

_____ 6. Role accumulation can be accomplished through role making.

_____ 7. Nancy Drew's daring and cleverness illustrates sex role pluralism.

_____ 8. Observational techniques in sociology illustrate a scientific paradigm.

_____ 9. The existence of a cultural paradigm implies that a culture has little or no unity.

_____10. Age role continuity tends to result in severe conflicts.

Concept Definition: Write the definition of the concept or term appearing on the left in the blank space next to it.

1. sex role pluralism _____

_____

2. chronological age _____

_____

3. age role _____

_____

4. age role pluralism _____

_____

5. disengagement theory _____

_____

6. cultural paradigm _____

_____

7. ageism _____

_____

8. role accumulation _____

_____

9. activity theory _____

10. age role continuity _____

_____

ANSWERS

Self Quiz

1.	c	6.	c	11.	a	16.	c
2.	a	7.	a	12.	d	17.	a
3.	d	8.	b	13.	b	18.	d
4.	d	9.	c	14.	c	19.	c
5.	b	10.	a	15.	b	20.	d

Concept Recognition

1. sexism
2. sex role
3. age role
4. age role discontinuity
5. gender

6. sex role pluralism
7. bracketing
8. disengagement theory
9. ageism
10. paradigm

True-False

1.	F	6.	T
2.	T	7.	T
3.	T	8.	F
4.	T	9.	F
5.	T	10.	F

Concept Definition

See Glossary in back of this booklet

The Family
10

OVERVIEW

Institutions are social structures that focus on
certain values (e.g., political institutions on power,
economic institutions on wealth). The family is an institution which provides for children's basic biological
needs and is very influential in socializing them. It
also structures intimate social (including sexual) relationships among adults. Goal displacement is a phenomenon which can help explain motivations of family
members. The "soap opera family" in American society
can help us to understand the way many people view
family life. Pluralistic family forms are a recent
trend in American society, such as the dual work family,
the single parent family, and the reconstituted (remarried with children) family.

SYNOPSIS

10.1 The Nature of Institutions

a Introduction

An institution is a social structure built on certain key values, such as power for the political institution and wealth for the economic institution. And
because values tend to persist, so do institutions. An

institution can be vast, such as religion in the
U.S., or it can be relatively narrow, such as Christ-
mas. The science fiction trilogy <u>Dune</u>, <u>Dune Messiah</u>,
and <u>Children of Dune</u> illustrates the great power
institutions exert over individuals. For example,
Paul's orientations are humanistic, yet he is swept
along in the role of Muad'Dib, the deity worshipped
by a religious cult that engulfs all the known
planets. A total institution cuts people off from
the wider society and enforces on them a formally
administered round of life, as exemplified by pri-
sons, mental hospitals and monasteries.

b Goal Displacement

John Wesley, who founded Methodism, wondered if it
is possible to prevent the spirit of Methodism
being replaced by "love of the world in all its
branches," since Methodism encourages the individual
to work hard, save, and grow rich. The replacement
of love of God by love of riches illustrates the
phenomenon of goal displacement. Such goal displacement may, in turn, be an "unanticipated consequence of purposive action. "Here, the purposive
action would be hard work and saving, and the unanticipated consequences would be a declining
interest in God or spiritual matters. There are
numerous examples of such unanticipated consequences throughout history, such as the absorption
by Christianity of an elitest orientation as a
result of the purposive alliance of the early
Christians with the Roman Empire. Goal displacement is encouraged by the very nature of institutions, since they generally teach us to think in
narrow ways.

10.2 <u>The Nature of the Family</u>

a Functions and Types of Families

Important functions which the family fulfills for
society include socializing the child, providing
for the child's basic biological needs, and helping
adults develop intimate social and sexual relationships. Two major types of families are the nuclear
family (parents and their children) and the extended family (two or more nuclear families and
three or more generations). If we take into account
the many different cultures throughout the world,
we find great variation among families. Thus,
living arrangements vary (patrilocal, matrilocal,

neolocal), the number of spouses varies (monogamy, polygyny, polyandry), and power in the family varies (patriarchal, matriarchal, equalitarian).

b   The Family in Traditional China

Hsu, in examining biographies of hundreds of individuals in a traditional Chinese community, noted that families tended to rise and fall very quickly; in only very few cases were both a father and a son eminent enough to have separate biographical entries. He concluded that rich sons become accustomed to a life of consumption, that the family subsequently loses its wealth, and that it takes another generation to develop the self discipline necessary to achieve wealth once again. This illustrates the phenomenon of goal displacement: the goals of consumption and hard work tend to displace one another.

c   The Family in Contemporary China

An excerpt from a contemporary Cantonese newspaper describing Chinese weddings illustrates the heavy emphasis of political ideology on hard work. This contrasts with the link between Protestantism and hard work in Western society. To the extent that it continues from one generation to the next, the goal displacement between consumption and hard work will no longer occur.

10.3 The Family and Industrialization

Earlier studies within sociology portrayed a picture of the family as having shifted as a result of the industrialization process from the extended to the nuclear type. Supposedly, the large family with three or more generations involved and several nuclear families was in a good position to cope with an agricultural life, given the usefulness of children for planting and harvesting. It was thought that, with the coming of industrialization, geographical mobility on the part of the work force was necessary if industry was to be adequately served, and a much smaller family therefore came into existence. Contemporary theory, however, has concluded that the nuclear family existed prior to industrialization and was one factor which helped in the origins of industrialization. It is now believed that there is a two-way relationship between industrialization and the nuclear family,

113

with each influencing the other.

10.4 The Family in the Mass Media

a The Soap Opera Family: The Role of Children

Goldsen, in a study of American soap operas, concludes that children are almost completely ignored,
and that pregnancy and birth are extremely risky
affairs. She believes that children are dismissed
with pious expressions of love that turn out to be
phony.

b The Child-Rearing Literature

The emphasis within popular child-rearing literature,
such as the various editions put out by Dr. Spock,
greatly vary with the period. Between 1820 and
1942, advice to parents was legitimized (justified)
largely on the basis of Christian theology along
with a stern morality. Between 1942 and 1968 there
was a turning away from religious guidance and
toward the ideas of Freud. And between 1968 and
1970 there has been another shift, this time away
from permissiveness and toward an attempt to recognize the importance of parental needs along with
those of the child.

c The Soap Opera Family: Relationships among Adults

Soap operas in the U.S. center on life's problems.
They are melodramas in that they endlessly dwell
on those problems. But at the same time, they tend
to be highly optimistic, as we may note from such
titles as Search for Tomorrow, Love of Life, and
The Brighter Day. Their focus is on the overriding
importance of achieving intimate relationships with
others.

10.5 The Contemporary American Family

a A Revolution of Rising Expectations?

The soaps alert us to the gap between our desires
for intimate relationships and our ability to
achieve such relationships. The "revolution of
rising expectations" in contemporary society is
an acceleration of aspirations. Even if our ful-
fillments or achievements remain stable, such an
acceleration can create large gaps between aspira-

114

tion and fulfillment, resulting in separation or
divorce. According to Farrell, this illustrates
the failure of good marriages, for good marriages
can raise our aspirations for even better marriages.

b Pluralistic Family Forms

In addition to our traditional nuclear family with
children and with only one career, a variety of
other kinds of families are becoming more and more
important: the two-career family, the nuclear
family without children, the single-parent family,
the reconstituted family (remarried nuclear family
with children), the communal family, and so on.

Multiple Choice: In the space provided, enter the letter of the answer that best completes the question.

_____ 1. An institution, organization and group are related in that

a) an organization is a type of group
b) an institution is a type of group
   c) a group is a type of institution
d) an institution is a type of organization

    c

_____ 2. A total institution and an institution are related in that

a) both are types of organizations
b) both are totalitarian
c) both are social structures
d) both are groups

_____ 3. When two variables change in opposite directions, this indicates

a) a direct relationship between two variables
b) an inverse relationship between two variables
c) both of the above
d) neither of the above

_____ 4. John Wesley, in referring to a decline in the spirit of Methodism,

a) blames the atheists and agnostics for this development
b) blames Catholicism for this development
c) blames Methodism itself for this development
d) blames science for this development

_____ 5. Goal displacement

a) always is produced by purposive action
b) may be a consequence of purposive action
c) refers to an emphasis on two goals rather than one
d) refers to a loss of goals

_____ 6. A historical illustration of unanticipated consequences of purposive action resulted from

a) Classical Athens neglecting to force obedience from small towns in its efforts to extend its empire
b) the refusal of the early Christians to ally the Church with the Roman Empire
c) Philip II's refusal to use the Inquisition to obtain obedience
d) the use of cattle prods by some Southern sheriffs to deprive blacks of their civil rights

7. A major reason for the unanticipated consequences of purposive action is that

a) institutions teach us to think in narrow ways
b) institutions are oriented around a very broad range of values
c) the political institution overlaps with the economic institution
d) the religious institution overlaps with the educational institution

8. Which of these is not a major function of the family for society:

a) satisfying and regulating the desires of adults for intimate social and sexual relationships
b) socializing the child
c) providing appropriate goal displacements
d) generating offspring

9. In which of these types of relationships is one woman the spouse of two or more men:

a) polygyny
b) monogamy
c) polygamy
d) polyandry

10. In the traditional Chinese family

a) the husband-wife relationship is subordinate to the parents-son relationship
b) a man is expected to take his wife's side in a quarrel with his parents
c) a woman's first duties are to her husband
d) the most important relationship is between mother and son

11. The rise and fall of the traditional Chinese family is in part the result of

   a) the role of politics in family affairs
   b) goal displacement
   c) the emphasis on hard work and saving money
   d) the change from one generation's emphasis on hard work to another generation's emphasis on saving money

12. In contemporary China, political orientations appear to

   a) de-emphasize marriage
   b) de-emphasize a wedding feast
   c) emphasize consumption and the importance of leisure
   d) emphasize the correctness of Confusius' and Lin Piao's ideas

13. The relationship between the family and industrialization in contemporary China may best be described by this statement:

   a) industrialization is changing the family from an extended to a nuclear one
   b) smaller families are developing because of industrial, political, educational and religious changes
   c) industrialization is reinforcing respect for the wishes of parents
   d) industrialization is strengthening the family's control over job opportunities

14. In the American soap opera family, the role of children

   a) is an important one
   b) is more realistic by far than the role of the adult
   c) is a minor one
   d) illustrates age role continuity

15. The American soap opera, in relation to family life,

   a) is melodrama associated with pessimism
   b) is melodrama emphasizing the importance of work
   c) is melodrama emphasizing the importance of

play
d) is melodrama emphasizing the importance of adults achieving intimate relationships

_____ 16. The 1968-1970 period reveals, with respect to popular child-rearing literature,

a) a concern for parental needs along with those of children
b) a relaxation of discipline
c) a return of the importance of control over masterbation
d) a return to the importance of early bowel training

_____ 17. In Mary Hartman, Mary Hartman, goal displacement is best illustrated by

a) baking better cakes in place of achieving sexual fulfillment
b) avoiding wax buildup when polishing the floor
c) Mary's being confined to a mental institution
d) the drowning of Mary's friend in a bowl of chicken soup

_____ 18. "Davies' theory of revolution" and "the revolution of rising expectations" are related in that

a) both refer to a decline in need-satisfactions
b) both refer to a rise in need-satisfactions as a basis for revolution
c) both refer to a rise in aspirations as a basis for revolution
d) both refer to a decline in performance

_____ 19. The reconstituted family

a) is the family in which the spouses divorce and then remarry one another
b) is the family which separates and then gets together again
c) is the family in which children leave and then come back to live with their parents (with or without their own spouses)
d) is the family made up of spouses, one or both of whom has been previously married

119

and has a child or children from that marriage

_____ 20. A communal family is one in which

   a) several nuclear families related by blood
      live together
   b) several nuclear families live together and
      share sexual relations
   c) several nuclear families related by blood
      live together and share sexual relations
   d) several nuclear families live together and
      share everything except sexual relations

Concept Recognition: Write the concept or term in the
blank space next to its definition.

_____ 1. The replacement of one goal or
value by another.

_____ 2. A social structure built around
certain values and tending to persist in time.

_____ 3. Results of goal-directed actions
that differ from original expectations.

_____ 4. A social structure made up of
people related by blood, marriage or adoption.

_____ 5. Several nuclear families usually
not related by blood living together and sharing
everything except sexual relations.

_____ 6. The justification of behavior
on the basis of cultural or subcultural values and
norms.

_____ 7. A family made up of parents and
their children.

_____ 8. A group deliberately constructed
to seek specific goals.

_____ 9. The replacement of one goal or
value by another.

_____ 10. A man and a woman, at least one
of whom has been previously married and has a child
or children from that prior marriage.

True/False: Enter "T" for true or "F" for false for the best answer to the statement.

_____ 1. Dune emphasizes the importance of mass formal education in over-turning a political institution.

_____ 2. A total institution is illustrated by a mental hospital.

_____ 3. An inverse relationship between two variables is one in which the variables change in the same direction.

_____ 4. In a neolocal family, husband and wife live with the wife's parents.

_____ 5. The relationship between industrialization and type of family is a two-way one.

_____ 6. According to Goldsen, if a daytime-soap-opera woman discovers that she's pregnant, the chances are seven out of ten either that she's not married to the father or that the pregnancy is not desired by one or both parents.

_____ 7. In the first decades of the twentieth century, popular child-rearing literature was legitimated on the basis of Christian theology.

_____ 8. The soap opera Mary Hartman, Mary Hartman, contains very little melodrama.

_____ 9. According to Farrell, good marriages can fail because they can raise aspirations.

_____10. In a group marriage, there is a sharing of everything except sexual relations.

Concept Definition: Write the definition of the concept or term appearing on the left in the blank space next to it.

1. total institution _____

_____

2. inverse relationship between two variables _____

_____

3. trial marriage _____

_____

4. two-career family _____

_____

5. direct relationship between two variables _____

_____

6. contract marriage _____

_____

7. single-parent family _____

_____

8. homosexual marriage _____

_____

9. group marriage _____

_____

10. group _____

_____

ANSWERS

Self Quiz

1.	a	6.	d	11.	b	16.	a
2.	c	7.	a	12.	b	17.	a
3.	b	8.	c	13.	b	18.	c
4.	c	9.	d	14.	c	19.	d
5.	b	10.	a	15.	d	20.	d

Concept Recognition

1. goal displacement
2. institution
3. unanticipated conse-
   quences of purposive
   action

6. legitimation
7. nuclear family
8. organization
9. extended family

4. family   10. reconstituted family
5. communal family

True-False

1. F   6.   T
2. T   7.   F
3. F   8.   F
4. F   9.   T
5. T   10.   F

Concept Definition

See Glossary in back of this booklet

Religion
11

OVERVIEW

   Religion is an institution coordinating theology, faith and ritual around problems of ultimate significance, such as birth, death, marriage and economic survival. Its influence is not dependent on a conscious commitment to a religious life or church attendance, and it pervades society as a whole (including the comic book Howard the Duck). The Protestant ethic, studied by Weber and more recently by Lenski, was important in the development of capitalism or industrialization in Western society, and it is still a basis for American values emphasizing activity and work.

SYNOPSIS

11.1 The Nature of Religion

   a Defining Religion: Theology, Faith, Ritual

      There are three essential aspects of religion: theology, faith, and ritual. Theology emphasizes a system of ideas, faith is deep emotional conviction, and ritual stresses the notion of repetitive actions at certain times. In Howard the Duck, theology is illustrated by a division of the world into the bad (such as Prodigal Can Co.) and the good (Howard and his followers). Howard expresses complete faith in his own ideas. Rituals are illustrated by the Jewish Passover seder and the Catholic mass. Religion is an institution-- a persistent social structure--coordinating theology, faith and ritual as a way of solving ultimate problems, such as the meaning of life and death.

b   Locating Religion in Society

Theology is expressed in places of work as well as in church, in comic books as well as in sacred texts such as the Talmud and the Koran. We find rituals at college commencement exercises as well as in synagogues. And faith is expressed within close human relationships just as it is in mosques. Religion is to be found throughout society, since we may think about, develop commitments concerning, and attempt to deal with ultimate problems in all aspects of life. Yet whether or not we recognize the fact, we are deeply influenced by the major religions developed in society (such as Catholicism, Protestantism, and Judaism).

c   The Sacred and the Profane

Durkheim's distinction between the sacred and the profane is illustrated by the way we generally dress and conduct ourselves in church, synagogue, temple or mosque: we are careful (in general) to show proper respect within a house of worship.by avoiding sports clothing or loud voices. This distinction is less useful for locating or defining religio- in the contemporary world than previously. Many individuals hold science, which tends to accept no assumption as sacred, with deep religious conviction.

11.2 Religion and Other Institutions

a   The Protestant Ethic and the Development of Capitalism

Weber's fundamental hypothesis is that the Protestant ethic (values emphasizing hard work and saving), which stems from Calvinistic theology, was a powerful force in the origin of capitalism. There is some question among economists and historians as to the correctness of this hypothesis, but such questions become less significant if we focus on

the role of the Protestant ethic in the development--
rather than the origin--of capitalism or the industrialization process.

b   The Protestant Ethic and Contemporary American
    Society

Lenski's analysis of a 1958 survey of Detroit residents concludes that the Protestant ethic continues to affect people's behavior. For example,
a higher percentage of white Protestants than Jews
or white Catholics rated work itself (along with
the feeling of accomplishment it gives) as being
more important than, say, high income or job secu-
rity.

c   Industrialization and Eastern Religion

Weber saw Confucianism and Buddhism as lacking
Protestantism's ability to motivate the individual
to achieve economic success and, thus, influence
the development of capitalism. According to Bellah,
the feudal Tokugawa period (1600-1868) in Japan
provided the basis for a revival of the ancient
Shinto religion, with its emphasis on loyalty to
the Emperor. And when the Emperor (Mikado) chose
the path of rapid industrialization, the Japanese
people loyally followed. However, other factors
also encouraged industrialization, such as the
zaibatsu or great industrial clans.

11.3 Religion and Goal Displacement

a   Goal Displacement within Religious Organizations

Among religious organizations there appears to be
continuing change: small sects that tend to conflict with existing churches become transformed
into large, conservative and relatively impersonal
churches. Moberg distinguishes among five stages
in this transition or "life cycle": (1) preliminary organization, (2) formal organization, (3) maximum efficiency, (4) institutional, and (5) disintegration. This shift is not inevitable and thus
can be stopped or reversed. It illustrates goal
displacement, in which the sect's original spiritual
values give way to the church's desire for a large
membership and the continuation of its organization.

b   Goal Displacement in Society

126

Goal displacement within society as a whole is illustrated by Lowenthal's analysis of the biographies
appearing in The Saturday Evening Post and Collier's
between 1901 and 1941. He found a displacement of
"idols of production" by "idols of consumption": a
smaller proportion from political life as well as
from business and the professions, and a larger
proportion from the entertainment world. However,
the Protestant work ethic still appears to be alive
in the United States; other observers have argued
that it has not yet been displaced.

114. Secularization

a Sacred and Secular

Becker distinguishes between the sacred society
and the secular society. The sacred society is
geographically and socially isolated, and change
is distrusted; it is a gemeinschaft or close community. The secular society is in close communication with the outside world, rapidly changing,
and is a gesellschaft or relatively impersonal
society.

b Contemporary Trends

Becker identifies a major historical trend: secularization, that is, movement from a sacred society
(emphasizing traditionalism and isolation) to a
secular society (emphasizing change, communication
and science). Sacrilization is, by contrast, movement toward a sacred society. Within religion,
secularization is illustrated by the "selling" of
religion as a path to personal adjustment, an idea
conveyed by Dr. Norman Vincent Peale's The Power
of Positive Thinking. The secularization of religion is illustrated in a different way by Erich
Fromm's emphasis on the value of "humanistic"
(oriented to helping human beings) as distinct from
"authoritarian" forms of religion; it is also illustrated by Fletcher's concept of "situation ethics."
Secularization can be influenced by a given "generation unit," such as the impact of young people
within the "counterculture" during the 1960s. Ber-
ger maintains that the plausibility structure (patterns of social relationships supporting a given
world-view) supporting the Christian view of the
world is diminishing, and there is evidence in
support of this hypothesis.

c Images of the Future

Science fiction portrays both negative images of
the future (dystopias) like Vonnegut's Player Piano
and positive images (utopias) like Star Trek books,
with the former tending to outnumber the latter.
Polak claims that the positive Judeo-Christian
image of a God or Other has powered the development
of Western civilization for over two thousand years,
but that we have lost faith in it. He believes
that, as a result, our future is threatened, since
images of the future help to create the future. He
suggests that we strive to develop a new positive
image of the future that can capture the collective
imagination.

SELF-QUIZ

Multiple Choice: In the space provided, enter the letter of the answer that best completes the question.

_____ 1. A theology

   a) is all that is needed for the development of a religion
   b) is not an essential part of religion
   c) cannot be a genuine theology without some recognition of the existence of some Being, Force or God
   d) none of the above

_____ 2. To define religion in terms of an emphasis on the sacred

   a) is just as inadequate as defining it on the basis of the existence of God
   b) is an approach that would result in including science as a kind of religion
   c) is relevant to contemporary approaches to religion more than traditional ones
   d) makes most sense when we understand the contemporary importance of science

_____ 3. Dr. Spock's advice on child-rearing

   a) has nothing to do with religion
   b) illustrates the phenomenon of ritual
   c) is part of the theology which a number of people believe
   d) is fundamental to the religion of Western society

_____ 4. The directors of the Prodigal Can Co., who manufacture non-returnable containers,

   a) are not acting in a religious way
   b) are not influenced by a genuine theology
   c) are probably influenced by religion
   d) are influenced by ritual rather than theology or faith

_____ 5. Goal displacement is best illustrated by

   a) a corporation developing a new product differing from the old one
   b) a synagogue shifting its location from one

corner to the next
c) a mosque modifying its hours for worship
d) a college eliminating small classes and
going after big government grants instead

6. A secular society is best illustrated by

a) governmental elimination of any form of
church worship
b) complete freedom of speech
c) ability to leave a country if threatened by
imprisonment for attempting to conduct
church services
d) harsh penalties for those who blow up computers

7. Sacrilization is best illustrated by

a) the jailing of film directors who criticize
the government
b) the expansion of churches and synagogues
and the loss of personal relationships
within these houses of worship
c) the development of television programs
with religious themes
d) the growth of interfaith feeling and joint
conferences among Catholics, Protestants
and Jews

8. The rise of the Protestant ethic

a) is an example of sacrilization
b) was accompanied by a trend toward secularization
c) illustrates the trend toward a sacred society
d) produced, ultimately, a decline of religion
in Western society

9. A generation unit is best illustrated by

a) community housing for the elderly
b) people who protest against abortion
c) young people who protested against the war
in Vietnam during the 1960s
d) people who believe in radically changing
our economic system

10. An example of a utopia is

a) the birth of a new generation unit
b) a view of the end of all plausibility structures for Christianity
c) a countercultural vision of a world where
   everyone is free to "do his own thing"
d) a vision of a decline in the humanistic
   perspective

_____ 11. Which one of these best illustrates religious
faith:

a) going to a Buddhist temple on days of
   special religious significance
b) belief that Moses received the Ten Commandments from God on Mount Sinai
c) continuing feelings of intense love for one's
   fellow human beings as the central basis
   for one's behavior
d) an understanding of how all phenomena relate
   to one another from a scientific perspective

_____ 12. Which one of these best illustrates a religious
orientation:

a) going to a house of worship on several special
   religious holidays during the year
b) participation twice a week in a women's
   consciousness-raising group as the major
   basis for changing one's relations to one's
   family as well as the world in general
c) a belief in God's existence
d) a feeling of joy at Christmastime

_____ 13. The institution of science is best illustrated
by

a) a fixed belief in the truth of the law of
   gravity
b) the acceptance once and for all of the assumption that there is no God
c) the opening up of all assumptions to question
d) a fixed belief in the experiment as, inevitably, the key research technique of
   science

_____ 14. An example of another kind of organization
than a church going through several of the
stages in the "life cycle of the church" that
lead to disintegration is:

a) a college starting out emphasizing close
   student-teacher relationships and later
   focusing on research grants to the neglect
   of teaching
b) a political party which many written rules
   and regulations eliminating most of these
   rules
c) a Rotary Club reducing the number of its
   committees
d) a business organization eliminating three
   levels of its hierarchy: executive, associate, and assistant vice presidents

_____ 15. In the view of most sociologists, the relation
          of the Protestant ethic to capitalism is that:

a) the ethic had little to do with the development of capitalism
b) the ethic encouraged the development of
   capitalism
c) the Protestant ethic was far less important
   than the Jewish ethic in the development
   of capitalism
d) Calvinism, with its emphasis on fatalism,
   could not have encouraged hard work

_____ 16. The debate over Weber's link between Protes-
          tantism and capitalism does <u>not</u> include the
          idea that

a) French Catholic preachers emphasized industry and frugality
b) Weber allowed for other factors than Protestantism in the origins of capitalism
c) the whole Protestant movement was involved
   in the rise of capitalism
d) early Protestant theology emphasized the
   importance of materialism

_____ 17. In Weber's view of Eastern religions,

a) Confucianism emphasizes adaptation to the
   world rather than making over the world
b) Confucianism's focus on feudal loyalty
   paved the way for industrialism
c) the Buddhist emphasis the <u>nirvana</u> frees
   the individual to devote attention to hard
   work
d) the Buddhist focus on the individual provides the basis for an orientation toward

personal achievement and success

_____ 18. Which of these does not illustrate secularization:

a) situation ethics
b) concern with maintaining traditional religious forms
c) declining plausibility structures for church religion
d) the growth of a humanistic perspective

_____ 19. Shinto religion in Japan appears to

a) encourage the development of industrialization
b) be quite separate from Japan's political system
c) focus on nirvana
d) focus on life after death rather than on this world

_____ 20. Some stages in the life cycle of the church are

a) sacred, secular
b) sacred, profane
c) formal organization, disintegration
d) sacrilization, secularization

Concept Recognition: Write the concept or term in the blank space next to its definition.

_____ 1. An organization designed to deal with the religious needs of the masses in society.

_____ 2. A negative image of the future.

_____ 3. An institution which coordinates theology or beliefs, faith or emotional expression, and ritual or actions, as solutions to problems of ultimate significance in society.

_____ 4. A society legitimating traditionalism and isolation.

_____ 5. An institution focusing on the continuing development of knowledge based on methods which accept no assumption as sacred.

_____ 6. A system of ideas about the
nature of society and the universe, and about what
should be the human being's relation to them.

_____ 7. A vision of a possible future
reality for society and the individual.

_____ 8. A group joined together in protest against existing religious organizations.

_____ 9. The patterns of social relationships which support a given world view or definition
of social reality.

_____10. Phenomena superior in dignity
and power to profane things, and profoundly differentiated from--often opposed to--them.

True/False: Enter "T" for true or "F" for false for the
best answer to the statement.

_____ 1. Religion has at least some impact on every
major aspect of society.

_____ 2. Religion is illustrated mainly by the theology,
faith and ritual expressed in houses of worship.

_____ 3. Max Weber emphasized the Calvinistic belief
in free will as a basis for economic success.

_____ 4. The movement from sect to church may be reversed.

_____ 5. Weekly church attendance in the United States
has been dropping since 1955.

_____ 6. A humanistic perspective is not foreign to the
Judeo-Christian tradition.

_____ 7. The only religion which has proved to be a
powerful force in the development of industrialization is Protestantism.

_____ 8. It is possible for both secularization and the
growth of a humanistic perspective to occur
in the same society.

_____ 9. An image of the future is illustrated by the
communist dream of a classless society.

_____10. Utopias appear to far outnumber dystopias in American science fiction.

Concept Definition: Write the definition of the concept or term appearing on the left in the blank space next to it.

1. faith _____

_____

2. generation unit _____

_____

3. goal displacement _____

_____

4. ritual _____

_____

5. secular society _____

_____

6. counterculture _____

_____

7. sacrilization _____

_____

8. the Protestant ethic _____

_____

9. humanistic _____

_____

10. secularization _____

_____

ANSWERS

Self Quiz

1.	d	6.	b	11.	c	16.	d
2.	a	7.	a	12.	b	17.	a
3.	c	8.	b	13.	c	18.	b
4.	c	9.	c	14.	a	19.	a
5.	d	10.	c	15.	b	20.	c

Concept Recognition

1. church
2. dystopia
3. religion
4. sacred society
5. science
6. theology
7. image of the future
8. sect
9. plausibility structure
10. sacred entities

True-False

1.	T	6.	T
2.	F	7.	F
3.	F	8.	T
4.	T	9.	T
5.	T	10.	F

Concept Definition

See Glossary in back of this booklet

Political and Economic Institutions 12

OVERVIEW

Power includes force, authority and influence, and
the political institution structures the development,
distribution and use of power. Existing theoretical
perspectives on power (power structure, power elite,
and pluralist) focus on the distribution and use of
power, but the development of power (as illustrated
by Gandhi's movement for the independence of India) is
also a vital topic. Similarly, the problem of the
production of wealth--and not just its distribution or
use--is central to our understanding of the economic
system. The "growth" versus "limits to growth" illustrates alternative attitudes to production; the "culture of poverty" concept is associated with distribution;
and the ideas of "conspicuous consumption" and "conspicuous leisure" have to do with use.

SYNOPSIS

12.1 The Political Institution

a   The Nature of Power

Machiavelli, in his advice to Italian princes,
suggested that both force and law should be used
in the interests of unifying Italy. To force and

law (or authority) we can add a third type of power: influence.

Force has to do with violence or the threat of violence, and its importance is emphasized by conflict theorists. It generally goes against many of the fundamental values in contemporary society, such as the importance of the individual personality. And it can easily result in goal displacement, for the continuing use of force can come to be seen as an end in itself. In the science fiction story Star Maker, some civilizations chose the risk of being destroyed by a "mad" empire over the almost certain destruction of their own values through goal displacement. They calculated that goal displacement would result from their own long-term use of force.

Authority, or power that is legitimated by values and norms, may be of several types. Charismatic authority is based on exceptional personal qualities, such as those of a Jesus Christ, Joan of Arc, Adolf Hitler or Jack Kennedy. Traditional authority is rule based on previous tried-and-true patterns of behavior. Examples are the customs which surrounded the obedience of serfs to their lords or which surround the obedience of children to parents. Legal authority is rule based on law or written regulations. It is wide-spread in contemporary industrialized societies, as illustrated by the obedience of all of us to traffic lights, stop signs, etc.

Influence is the ability to achieve control over others beyond any authority to do so. Advertising has the power to affect our everyday decisions and propaganda can influence our ways of thinking. Leaders such as heads of business firms who may have no great charismatic or legal authority may nevertheless have considerable influence over others simply because of their positions.

b   The Distribution and Use of Power

The political institution has to do with the development, distribution and use of power. Concerning distribution and use, there are three major approaches to power: power structure, power elite, and pluralist.

The ideas of Karl Marx were most important in the origins of the power structure approach. This approach centers on economic stratification and the struggle between social classes in different economic situations. According to Marxist thinking, we must not be misled by such things as widespread voting into thinking that power is widely distributed. Economic power operates behind the scenes to exert its controls and political forms are merely a way of hiding what actually goes on.

The power elite approach was constructed by C. Wright Mills. It, too, emphasizes the stratification system, but it distinguishes different kinds of stratification: for example, based on wealth, based on status, based on leadership positions. Mills traced a number of careers to show how individuals who were high in one area easily moved into top positions in other areas (such as the former admiral who is appointed president of a huge corporation, or the celebrity who becomes a politician). For Mills, major power is held by a small group of such individuals. The pluralist approach comes closest to widespread beliefs about the way democracy works. There is--according to David Riesman--competition among different elites so that no one elite attains dominance. They function as "veto groups": each one checks the others. The result can easily lead to a power vacuum, with the power to stop others but not to initiate action.

c   The Development of Power

None of the foregoing approaches to power centers on how new power is developed. Their concern, rather, is with who has the power that already exists and how they use that power. We might see this as a focus on a "fixed pie of power" where concern lies with how the pie is sliced up. This is distinct from the notion of an "expanding pie of power," with the key question being how it expands.

Gandhi's techniques of conflict through communication--designated by the term Satyagraha--illustrate the idea of the development of power. He was able to achieve the end of independence of India from the United Kingdom by techniques in which his rivals were not humiliated and, overall, there were gains for Britain along with the gains for India. An

139

independent India, for example, continued to maintain its cultural ties with Britain, continued to
trade with her, and continued to follow the general
political system illustrated by her. For all this,
Britain no longer needed to maintain a large military force in India.

12.2 The Economic Institution

a The Production of Wealth

The economic institution centers on the production,
distribution and use of wealth. This parallels the
political institution's focus on the development,
distribution and use of power. Wealth is here
viewed as including nonmaterial or intangible goals
like feelings of inner harmony or wisdom.

The "revolution of rising expectations" is a major
factor in the production of wealth. Increased desire
for wealth provides would-be producers with a ready
market to sell their wares. And these "wares" are
services as well as goods, for we desire more intimate relationships with others as well as shiny
new cars. Problems of pollution and overpopulation have, in recent years, encouraged serious
questioning of our growth policies. The book,
Limits to Growth, illustrates such questioning
and makes dire predictions about our future unless
immediate steps are taken to achieve a plateau in
our production of goods. Similarly, a British
economist (Schumacher) has argued in Small Is
Beautiful that small technologies can replace
gigantic ones and that we should be paying attention to personal and social development in the
factory.

b Division of Labor

Our division of labor--the way specialized tasks
are organized around work goals--is central to our
economy. It has been associated with an industrial
system that has somehow managed to produce an enormous amount of wealth. Yet that division of labor
would probably be assessed by Durkheim as largely
"abnormal": the various specialists tend to know
little about one another's work, and they generally
have little understanding or interest in the overall
goals of their enterprises. As a result, the worker
in many ways is working as a kind of machine or a

cog in a huge machine.

c Hierarchy

Hierarchy in society as a whole is structured by
the social stratification system, and we see it in
the organization of work. We also see it in the
differences in the way of life of poor people as
distinct from others. Economic poverty does not
necessarily produce isolation, dependence and hopelessness. For example, poor students who believe
that this condition is temporary do not generally
develop a "culture of poverty." A culture (or subculture) of poverty becomes a powerful force which
tends to keep people in economic poverty. There
is, then, a vicious circle of factors which is not
easy to break if we wish to help people out of poverty.

Turning to the well-to-do segment of contemporary
society, we may note such phenomena as conspicuous
leisure and conspicuous consumption. Conspicuous
leisure is the avoidance of productive work as a
symbol of status, and conspicuous consumption is
the waste or use of valued goods as a means of
gaining status. These aspects of some people's
style of life affect their political power.

SELF-QUIZ

Multiple Choice: In the space provided, enter the letter of the answer that best completes the question.

_____ 1. Machiavelli's distinctions between two different aspects of power have to do most directly with the distinctions between

a) influence and authority
b) authority and force
c) authority and influence
d) force and influence

_____ 2. The Star Maker provides an illustration of actions based on

a) the fear of goal displacement
b) authority
c) charismatic authority
d) traditional authority

_____ 3. Influence is best illustrated by

a) the use of the voting booth
b) the hiring of minority-group workers
c) the television commercial
d) the passing of legislation by Congress

_____ 4. The break-in at Democratic National Headquarters in the Watergate Hotel best illustrates

a) force
b) influence
c) traditional authority
d) charismatic authority

_____ 5. The pluralist approach to power is best illustrated by the work of

a) Karl Marx
b) Sergei Eisenstein
c) C. Wright Mills
d) David Riesman

_____ 6. In the power structure approach to power, the state is viewed as

a) one among several major centers of power
b) a committee for managing the affairs of the

wealthy or owners
c) making decisions on the basis of competing
pressures from numerous interest groups
d) the major center of power in society

7. The film <u>Potemkin</u> best illustrates which approach to power:

a) power elite
b) pluralist
c) veto groups
d) power structure

8. In the power elite approach to power,

a) the elites act like veto groups
b) the various elites compete for power
c) one elite made up of individuals at the top of different hierarchies is at the inner core of power
d) owners of the means of production make up the power elite

9. Which of these does not illustrate scarcity of power:

a) the discovery of ways to achieve more intimate social relationships
b) the rise of the proletariat in place of the bourgeoisie
c) the tapping of more energy from the sun without damage to the environment
d) the elimination of cancer with no side-effects

10. Gandhi's <u>Satyagraha</u> techniques include

a) hiding one's intentions from the rival group
b) attempting to humiliate the rival group
c) refraining from violence toward the rival group
d) avoiding personal interaction with members of the rival group

11. Gandhi's <u>Satyagraha</u> campaigns

a) achieved charismatic authority over the British troops
b) compromised on all principles
c) were based on force

143

d) achieved widespread influence in Britain

_____ 12. The economic and political institutions are related in that

    a) both focus on wealth
    b) both focus on power
    c) both have to do with the distribution of something
    d) both emphasize material phenomena

_____ 13. The revolution of rising expectations is related to the production of wealth in that

    a) aspirations can motivate people to work hard
    b) achievements can rise despite aspirations
    c) out of revolutions come major changes
    d) when expectations fall, production may rise once again

_____ 14. The book, Limits to Growth,

    a) suggests that material growth should be limited
    b) suggests that nonmaterial growth should be limited
    c) both of the above
    d) neither of the above

_____ 15. Schumacher, in Small Is Beautiful, suggests that

    a) the problem of production has been solved
    b) enormous quantities of goods are not harmful
    c) work should enable people to develop their abilities as well as their relationships with others
    d) none of the above

_____ 16. Ellul, in The Technological Society, argues that

    a) we need far more emphasis on technology than presently exists
    b) methods or techniques presently dominate society
    c) wealth is a direct result of the industrialization process
    d) machines should replace people on the as-

144

sembly line to give the individual more leisure

_____ 17. In a normal division of labor, according to Durkheim,

a) specialists are necessarily involved in highly repetitive tasks
b) meaningless work is unavoidable
c) specialists are aware of one another's work
d) specialization is not a source of organic solidarity

_____ 18. For **Durkheim**, organic and mechanical solidarity are related in that

a) they are associated with different stages of the industrial revolution
b) both are associated with a preindustrial society
c) both are associated with an industrial society
d) both are associated with a postindustrial society

_____ 19. The "culture of poverty" concept has been criticized because

a) of its emphasis on how easily people can move out of poverty
b) it is too traditional
c) its author has done no research
d) it lumps together people from many different cultures

_____ 20. Conspicuous consumption is best illustrated by

a) the homemaker who is not in the labor force
b) the artist who becomes famous
c) the use of rare carpets and tapestries
d) backbiting gossip about who is and is not important

Concept Recognition: Write the concept or term in the blank space next to its definition.

_____ 1. The social structure centering on the development, distribution and use of power.

_____ 2. Rule based on belief in the
extraordinary personal qualities of the ruler.

_____ 3. The ability to control the
behavior of others beyond any authority to do so.

_____ 4. A culture arising from economic
poverty and characterized by isolation, dependence
and hopelessness.

_____ 5. Feelings of togetherness based
on a division of labor.

_____ 6. Physical coercion or the threat
of such coercion.

_____ 7. Rule based on conformity to
established modes of behavior.

_____ 8. The social structure centering
on the production, distribution and use of wealth.

_____ 9. High degree of communication
among specialists.

_____10. An orientation which views
power as stemming primarily or exclusively from
stratification in terms of wealth.

True/False: Enter "T" for true or "F" for false for the
best answer to the statement.

_____ 1. Charismatic, traditional and legal authority
            cannot all be present in the same leader.

_____ 2. The act of voting for President of the U.S.
            illustrates influence more than authority.

_____ 3. The power elite approach is illustrated by
            the work of C. Wright Mills.

_____ 4. The power structure approach is implicitly
            embodied within the U.S. Constitution.

_____ 5. Adopting an attitude of trust toward the rival
            group is part of Gandhi's approach to Satya-
            graha.

_____ 6. Civil disobedience is always an act of force.

_____ 7. Wealth includes material, but not nonmaterial, things in society.

_____ 8. The "overdeveloped" society, according to Mills, is dominated by a materialistic approach to life.

_____ 9. Blauner's studies of industrial life emphasize fragmentation along with a sense of isolation and powerlessness.

_____10. Conspicuous leisure is illustrated by the married woman who does not work and has employees to run the household.

Concept Definition: Write the definition of the concept or term appearing on the left in the blank space next to it.

1. wealth _____

_____

2. revolution of rising expectations _____

_____

3. traditional authority _____

_____

4. conspicuous consumption _____

_____

5. abnormal division of labor _____

_____

6. power _____

_____

7. pluralist approach to power _____

_____

8. power elite approach _____

_____

9. division of labor _____

_____

10. authority _____

_____

ANSWERS

Self Quiz

1.	b	6.	b	11.	d	16.	b
2.	a	7.	d	12.	c	17.	c
3.	c	8.	c	13.	a	18.	a
4.	a	9.	b	14.	a	19.	d
5.	d	10.	c	15.	c	20.	c

Concept Recognition

1. political institution
2. charismatic authority
3. influence
4. culture of poverty
5. organic solidarity
6. force
7. legal authority
8. economic institution
9. normal division of labor
10. power structure approach

True-False

1.	F	6.	F
2.	F	7.	F
3.	T	8.	T
4.	F	9.	T
5.	T	10.	T

Concept Definition

See Glossary in back of this booklet

Education

13

OVERVIEW

Educational stratification exists in the United
States as well as throughout the world. For example,
the Coleman study concluded that blacks in public schools
generally have less adequate facilities than whites (in
the U.S.). Such stratification is based on a great many
factors in addition to academic ability. For example,
Pygmalion in the Classroom showed that younger students
whose teachers were told that they were "late bloomers"
(but actually chosen at random) substantially improved
their IQ scores over students not so identified. Educational stratification is legitimated by myths emphasizing
the importance of sorting procedures. The idea of educational development is the product of such thinkers as
John Dewey, Ivan Illich and Paulo Freire. Dewey's progressive approach is the foundation for many attempts
at educational innovation, and has influenced Illich
and Freire among others.

SYNOPSIS

13.1 Education and Stratification

a   Stratification in American Society

Education is set up as a separate institution in

industrial, as distinct from preindustrial societies.
This is partly in response to the requirement that
students learn the highly specialized knowledge
used in any given area of society. Sociologists
have been interested in the degree of educational
achievement existing for different ethnic groups,
since the educational institution is crucial for
upward mobility in society. The long-run trend
has been toward greater equality. For example,
between 1950 and 1975 the percentage of blacks
completing high school or additional schooling more
than tripled, as distinct from a near-doubling for
whites.

In 1965 the Coleman Report found educational facilities for blacks in the public schools to be infer-
ior to those for whites. Further, family background was seen as the greatest determinant of
academic performance. Also, pupil achievement was
found to be related to the educational background
and aspirations of other students in the same school.
The latter conclusion suggested that a white
majority in a school would help black students,
and busing to achieve that ratio has been instituted
in many places. Yet as of 1973 minority group en-
rollments were over 50 percent for two-thirds of
the twenty largest U.S. cities. In a review of
studies on the racial composition of schools, St.
John noted mixed results. For example, desegregation has sometimes raised achievement scores of
black children, but it also may have negative effects
on the self-esteem of black children in the short run.

b   Stratification in Other Societies

Two types of mobility are contest mobility, characteristic of patterns in the U.S., and sponsored
mobility, typical of British and Israeli patterns.
In the former, no early decision is made as to how
far the individual will go educationally; rather,
this is determined as a result of a series of open
"contests" such as examinations. In the latter,
an early decision is made, usually on the basis of
an examination, to give or withhold elite status
from the individual.

c   Educational Ideals: Meritocracy Versus Egalitar-
ianism

An educational meritocracy is an educational system with merit--as determined by academic performance--as the basis for advancement, thus providing equal opportunity for all students. Studies show that a number of factors affect student educational attainments, such as parents' educational attainment and the number of books in the home. Thus, "merit" appears to be affected by factors over which the student has no control, since those factors affect academic performance. The ideal of a meritocracy, further, differs from the ideal of equality of attainment.

d Stratification in the School and Classroom

According to Kamens, myths pervade the U.S. educational system, such as the idea that Ivy League colleges are actually better because they are so selective. Another illustration is the idea that college graduates are superior to nongraduates. Emphasis on credentials, Kamens believes, can be harmful. He maintains that schools teach society who is and who is not educated rather than actually educate people in important ways.

The power of definitions of the situation is further suggested by Rosenthal's Pygmalion in the Classroom. In this experiment with an elementary school, one-fifth of the student body was picked at random and designated as "late bloomers" to the teachers, who thought that the designation was based on a new kind of test. The "late bloomers" (the experimental group) improved their IQ scores during the academic year significantly more than did the other students (the control group). This occurred for grades 1 and 2, but not for later grades. Results may be interpreted in terms of a self-fulfilling prophesy, in which a prediction about a child's future performance is itself a major factor in the accuracy of the prediction. Since the control group also generally improved in IQ, we might suspect the operation of the Hawthorne effect. This is the improvement of performance as a result of scientific research of scientific research (which might have given a boost to morale at the school).

13.2 Educational Development

a Counterculture and Education

151

Beyond our examination of the distribution of educational rewards, we can also examine the factors which help to "develop" the individual educationally and, thus, make for a quality education. How deeply does education affect the child, and what makes for depth? Aspects of American student counterculture of the 1960s called for a good deal of depth, that is, resocialization of the individual through education. Another orientation of counterculture (a culture focused on opposition to the prevailing culture) was a reaction against science, as illustrated by the comic book, <u>Dr. Strange: Master of Black Magic</u>.

b   John Dewey: Progressive Education

John Dewey, along with others such as Charles Peirce and George Herbert Mead, helped to develop the philosophy of pragmatism. In this philosophy, there is a focus on the impact of ideas, science and man being a central place in the modern world. Dewey saw "progressive education" as working in this direction with an emphasis on developing the student's individuality as well as on learning through experience. Knowledge of the past is also important, but it must be made relevant to the present. Recent research on progressive education in Britain concludes that formal teaching methods have particular advantages in certain situations over purely informal ones. American sociologists have pointed up the importance of large-scale factors operating outside of the classroom on the quality of education inside the classroom, such as the needs of the economic system.

c   Ivan Illich: Should Attendance Be Compulsory?

Ivan Illich, who taught in Latin America for many years, believes that compulsory education tends to increase the student's dependence by placing her or him at the bottom of the educational hierarchy. He refers to this as the "schooling" of the individual. Students learn a "hidden curriculum": that they are incompetent to learn on their own. And Illich believes that this same lesson is taught in all other institutions.

d   Paulo Freire: The Culture of Silence

Ivan Illich also taught for many years in Latin America, focusing on peasants. He and his co-workers would go into an area and attempt to learn the key words and problems of those living there so as to give him the basis for developing student motivation. Discussions of a word such as "government" can give students some understanding of their potential power to "transform the world" and move out of the "culture of silence." Freire's ideals are related to those of Dewey and Illich, and his specific technique suggest some ways to achieve them.

SELF-QUIZ

Multiple Choice: In the space provided, enter the letter
of the answer that best completes the question.

_____ 1. Education in preindustrial society

a) is generally institutionalized
b) requires lengthy study
c) generally is not coordinated within one
   relatively stable social structure
d) is essential to impart bodies of highly
   specialized knowledge in preparation for
   specialized work in society

_____ 2. The Supreme Court's <u>Brown</u> decision of 1954
            declared that

a) separate educational facilities are inher-
   ently unequal
b) separate educational facilities are in almost all cases unequal
c) separate educational facilities are in most
   cases unequal
d) separate educational facilities are frequently unequal

_____ 3. According to the Coleman Report on American
            education, based on a 1965 study, the most
            important determinant of academic performance
            is

a) the racial composition of his or her school
b) the quality of instruction
c) physical facilities, including libraries
   and textbooks available
d) family background

_____ 4. The racial composition of a school is viewed
            as important because

a) black children tend to achieve more in pre-
   dominantly white schools
b) black children tend to achieve more in
   schools which are 25 percent white
c) black children tend to achieve less in
   schools that are almost completely white
d) none of the above

_____ 5. St. John's review of the impact of biracial schooling suggests that

    a) white achievement tends to be unaffected in schools that remain majority white
    b) white achievement tends to drop in majority black schools
    c) both of the above
    d) neither of the above

_____ 6. Sponsored mobility is characteristic of

    a) the U.S.
    b) Israel
    c) both of the above
    d) neither of the above

_____ 7. An educational meritocracy stresses

    a) equality of educational attainment
    b) equality of educational opportunity
    c) an end to stratification in education
    d) an end to the stratified class society

_____ 8. Kamens' analysis of American education implies that

    a) credentialism is a serious problem
    b) it is no myth that Ivy League colleges are genuinely superior
    c) it is no myth that college graduates are genuinely superior to nongraduates
    d) it is no myth that colleges genuinely control the learning experiences of students

_____ 9. Trained incapacity is best illustrated by

    a) the teaching profession
    b) the legal profession
    c) nurses learning to avoid contact with patients
    d) mathematicians learning how to write for journals

_____ 10. Rosenthal's _Pygmalion in the Classroom_ includes the finding that

    a) "late bloomers" did better than the control group for grades 5 and 6
    b) "late bloomers" did better than the control

group for grades 3 and 4
c) the control group generally lowered their
   IQ scores
d) the control group generally raised their
   IQ scores

_____ 11. The Rosenthal study, Pygmalion in the Classroom, suggests that

a) a Hawthorne effect might have taken place
b) no Hawthorne effect could possible have
   occurred
c) teachers may be more interested in working
   with older children
d) the self-fulfilling prophesy does not apply
   to this study

_____ 12. The American student counterculture of the
1960s was oriented to

a) the use of science to achieve enlightenment
b) the use of technology for more effective
   education
c) the class struggle between capitalism and
   socialism
d) a focus on self exploration as a basis for
   resocialization

_____ 13. Galbraith sees which conflict as becoming important in American society:

a) capital and labor
b) the individual personality and the organization
c) the "haves" and the "have-nots"
d) women and men

_____ 14. Dr. Strange (the comic book) best illustrates

a) the effectiveness of modern medicine
b) alternatives to science
c) the power of wealth
d) the importance of formal education

_____ 15. Which of the following is not associated with
the development of the philosophy of pragmatism:

a) George Herbert Mead
b) Charles Pierce
c) Lewis Coser

d) John Dewey

_____ 16. Saint Exupery's <u>The Little Prince</u> best illustrates

   a) the importance of traditional education
   b) the importance of science
   c) investigator effect
   d) disrespect for the child as a unique individual

_____ 17. According to Dewey's ideas,

   a) there must be explicit rules within the school
   b) knowledge of the past is unimportant
   c) traditional education is of no real value
   d) we must learn to think in either-or terms

_____ 18. British researchers have found in comparing formal with informal teaching methods that

   a) formal teaching methods are not as effective in creative areas
   b) formal teaching methods hurt the child's emotional development
   c) formal teaching methods are superior for teaching basic skills
   d) formal teaching methods harm the child's social development

_____ 19. Ivan Illich believes that

   a) the political institution teaches people dependency on authorities
   b) compulsory education is essential for industrial societies
   c) the educational institution does not teach people dependency
   d) the religious institution does not teach people dependency

_____ 20. Paulo Freire believes that

   a) teachers should not try to learn while teaching
   b) illiterate peasants require a long period of formal schooling
   c) a systematic classroom structure makes motivation of students unnecessary
   d) teachers should learn the vocabulary that

students actually use.

Concept Recognition: Write the concept or term in the blank space next to its definition.

_____ 1.   A subculture that is focused on opposition to the prevailing culture in society as a whole.

_____ 2.   An educational system with equal opportunity for all students to rise on the basis of academic performance.

_____ 3.   The development of a more favorable self-image, along with behavior appropriate to that image, based on changes in the expectations of significant others.

_____ 4.   The social structure that emphasizes the communication of knowledge.

_____ 5.   A pattern of accepting formal symbols of educational achievement as proof of actual educational achievement.

_____ 6.   A system of education stressing the cultivation of individuality, spontaneous student activities, learning through experience, and the importance of understanding the changing world.

_____ 7.   Improvement in performance based on the impact of scientific research.

_____ 8.   A pattern of educational mobility in which the individual is given elite status by the established elite on the basis of some criterion of supposed merit, usually applied at an early age.

_____ 9.   The learning of skills which obstruct their manifest purpose.

_____10.   A culture characterized by a lack of self-expression in thought or speech.

True/False: Enter "T" for true or "F" for false for the best answer to the statement.

_____ 1.   Between 1950 and 1975, a difference of 20 percent or more between U.S. blacks and whites completing high school or beyond persisted.

_____ 2. Coleman's recent (1976) conclusion is that various factors may negate the benefits of desegregation for black achievement.

_____ 3. Ethnic stratification does not tend to produce educational inequalities.

_____ 4. Contest mobility does not result in goal displacement.

_____ 5. According to most studies, the U.S. has achieved an educational meritocracy.

_____ 6. Trained incapacity is illustrated by "the higher illiteracy" of some Ph.D.'s in English.

_____ 7. Kamens' analysis of U.S. education suggests the dysfunctions of credentialism.

_____ 8. The Pygmalion effect is illustrated by the general decline in ability to construct grammatical statements in the U.S.

_____ 9. There is evidence that American universities are becoming more and more dependent upon the federal government for financial support.

_____10. Illich believes that "schooling" of the individual is harmful.

Concept Definition: Write the definition of the concept or term appearing on the left in the blank space next to it.

1. traditional education _____

_____

2. the Pygmalion effect _____

_____

3. sponsored mobility _____

_____

4. pragmatism _____

_____

5. institutionalization _____

_____

6. credentialism _____

_____

7. counterculture _____

_____

8. contest mobility _____

_____

9. educational meritocracy _____

_____

10. investigator effect _____

_____

ANSWERS

Self Quiz

1.	c	6.	b	11.	a	16.	d
2.	a	7.	b	12.	d	17.	a
3.	d	8.	a	13.	b	18.	c
4.	a	9.	c	14.	b	19.	a
5.	c	10.	d	15.	c	20.	d

Concept Recognition

1. counterculture
2. educational meritocracy
3. the Pygmalion effect
4. educational institution
5. credentialism
6. progressive education
7. the Hawthorne effect
8. sponsored mobility
9. trained incapacity
10. culture of silence

True-False

1.	T	6.	T
2.	T	7.	T
3.	F	8.	F
4.	F	9.	T
5.	F	10.	T

Concept Definition

See Glossary in back of this booklet

Groups and Organizations

14

OVERVIEW

Groups may be very small, such as the face-to-face primary group, or very large, as in multi-national corporations, communities and societies. Organizations (utilitarian, voluntary, and coercive) are deliberately put together for particular purposes, as illustrated by Enrico Fermi's research group at the University of Rome in the late 1920s and 1930s. Bureaucracies--organizations with extensive hierarchies and minute divisions of labor governed by explicit rules--exist in all institutions (perhaps with the exception of the family). They have important functions, such as providing continuity and direction, as well as dysfunctions, such as their fostering of the phenomenon of alienation.

SYNOPSIS

14.1 Groups

a   The Nature of the Group

Groups--which include such diverse entities as two-person relationships as well as entire societies-- differ from aggregates and social categories. A group consists of people who define themselves, or are defined by others, as a group, and who are in-

volved (directly or indirectly) in social relationships with one another. An aggregate is simply a
bunch of people congregated together, as the audience for a football game; a social category consists
of people classified together due to some common
characteristic, such as age or sex.

b Groups and Deviant Behavior

The Provo Experiment for rehabilitating delinquents
gave great responsibility to the incoming delinquent's peer group to help reform him, illustrating
the enormous power groups can wield over the individual. Those groups were oriented to learning
how to lead a straight life, and--by and large--
they were able to help the incoming delinquents to
do likewise.

c Primary and Secondary Groups

Charles Cooley, whose ideas like "the looking-glass
self" contributed to our understanding of socialization, developed the concept of the primary group:
a face-to-face group that is fundamental in the socialization process, such as the family. The secondary group, by contrast, generally does not have
deep emotional ties (such as students in a class).
The transition of societies to the development of
organic solidarity as well as the gesellschaft is
also a transition to an emphasis on secondary groups.

14.2 Organizations

a Utilitarian Organizations

An organization is a special kind of group: one
that is deliberately constructed to seek specific
goals. For example, there is the utilitarian organ-
ization--such as business organizations or univer-
sities--which people join in order to gain important personal benefits. Enrico Fermi's research
group, formed in the late 1920s at the University
of Rome, illustrates how effective such organizations can be and what makes them so effective. The
group created the technological basis for releasing
atomic energy. Many factors were involved, including
Fermi's personality (breadth of ideas as well as
sensitivity to his own emotions), his personal relationship with an Italian senator, a group of co-
workers with overlapping interests as well as genuine

163

emotional ties, the equalitarian orientation within the group, and its small size.

b   Voluntary Organizations

People join voluntary organizations because they are in sympathy with the organization's goals. Such organizations are extremely diverse, as illustrated by the Iceland Veterans and the Appalachian Mountain Club. Currently, voluntary organizations in the U.S. are in financial difficulties due in part to tax trends and the numerous appeals many individuals receive. The goals of voluntary associations reflect the "revolution of rising expectations."

c   Coercive Organizations

In a coercive organization--like a prison or a mental hospital--membership is obtained or maintained by force. Such organizations often perform "degredation ceremonies," which strip their recruits of key aspects of their personalities in an effort to resocialize them in part. Such organizations tend to be "total institutions" which segregate their members from society and treat them to a formally administered round of life.

d   An Analogy: The "Personality" of Organizations

Thurman Arnold attempted in 1937 to develop "a science of organizations, putting forward a number of interesting hypotheses. His fundamental idea is that an analogy drawn between the organization and the human personality can be highly suggestive. For example, any organization--like any personality-- has a unique character, is difficult to change, and is affected by the beliefs of those who surround it.

14.3 Bureaucracy

a   The Nature of Bureaucracy

Some organizations have an extensive hierarchy and division of labor and are governed by explicit rules; these are bureaucratic organizations, or bureaucracies. Max Weber described the "ideal type" or pure case of a bureaucracy, highlighting a list of key features which only occur in a real bureaucracy to some degree. These include rules giving it continuity, the principle of hierarchy among roles, administrators who are not owners, acts and rules recorded in writing, and so on.

b   Functions of Bureaucracy

Bureaucracy tends to have a bad reputation, yet it fulfills vital functions, as illustrated by Orson Welles' The Trial (an adaptation of the Kafka novel). Joseph K is accused of a serious crime but never told the nature of that crime nor allowed to confront his accusers. He is found guilty and sentenced in some unknown way to death, in part because he was unwilling to fawn on his lawyer who supposedly had influence with the judge. Bureaucratic rules, if they had existed, would have guaranteed to K some measure of fairness and openness in the entire proceedings.

c   Dysfunctions of Bureaucracy

Among the many complaints against bureaucracy is that it tends to limit the scope of the individual's personal development, that it is mired down with red tape and inefficiency, and that it rules become rigid and inhuman ends in themselves. Bureaucracy tends to encourage formal rationality, or decisions on the basis of criteria which can be readily quantified or calculated (such as in monetary terms). By contrast, the development and use of substantive rationality, in which decisions are based on a variety of ultimate ends (often humanistic and not easily quantifiable, such as happiness or fairness), tends to be neglected.

d   Formal and Informal Structures

Blau's study of a state employment agency in which interviewers violated many of the explicit organizational rules and goals (the formal structure) illustrates the power of an organization's informal structure (or its actual pattern of behavior, values and norms). Without the informal structure, fewer placements would have been made; thus, this structure was in part functional. But the informal structure tended to ignore counseling interviews, and this illustrates one of its dysfunctional results.

14.4 Alienation

a   The Nature of Alienation

Alienation refers to a sense of powerlessness, mean-ingless and social isolation associated with some kinds of social relationships, such as working on an assembly line or in a job where the tasks are undemanding and repetitive. It constrasts with involvement or commitment, such as is involved in the Buddhist perspective on work. Lang's film, Metropolis, portrays conditions producing aliena-tion: workers moving robot-fashion in an under-ground city.

b   Some Studies of Alienation

Research on alienation in the U.S. has uncovered diverse facts: large proportions of workers do not feel free to leave their place of work for as much as a half-hour, many find their work dull and monotonous, and unskilled workers tend to be more alienated than skilled workers. Automation, while changing some conditions that produce alienation, has fostered others. Overall, alienation appears to be a widespread and serious problem.

c   Indirect Illustrations of Reactions to Alienation:
    Comic-Book Heroes

Superman, Spiderman, Thor and Dr. Strange--comic book heroes--all have unusual abilities. Why do children and many adults follow their adventures? One possible explanation is that they provide what their viewers lack in everyday life: a sense of meaning, and power over events, providing a tempor-ary release from feelings of alienation.

d   Some Sources of Alienation

Organizations, and bureaucratic organizations in particular, have highly explicit and narrow goals, and these limit the scope of life for those working within them. The alienation accompanying this can be relieved by informal structures, but these are seen as illegitimate by the organization. "Job enlargement" illustrates one effort to counter alienation.

SELF-QUIZ

Multiple Choice: In the space provided, enter the letter of the answer that best completes the question.

_____ 1. Organizations, groups and institutions are related in that

a) institutions and organizations are types of groups
b) organizations and groups are types of institutions
c) all are systems of shared beliefs, interests and social relationships
d) groups are types of organizations

_____ 2. Groups, aggregates and social categories are related in that

a) they all have to do with collections or sets of people
b) groups and social categories refer to people involved in social relationships
c) aggregates and social categories refer to people involved in social relationships
d) aggregates and social categories are face-to-face groupings

_____ 3. The Provo delinquency experiment illustrates the idea that

a) new psychotherapeutic techniques can be effective
b) a well-planned orientation program is crucial
c) individual counseling can make a great difference
d) the delinquent's peer group can exert a very powerful influence

_____ 4. Primary and secondary groups are related in that

a) both are face-to-face
b) a small number of individuals is involved in both
c) both of the above
d) neither of the above

5. An organization and a bureaucracy are related in that

   a) both are necessarily utilitarian or coercive
   b) both are groups deliberately constructed to seek specific goals
   c) people join both because of shared goals
   d) both are generally dysfunctional for society

6. Secondary groups tend to

   a) promote mechanical solidarity
   b) be found in industrial society
   c) be found in a gemeinschaft
   d) be found in preindustrial society

7. In Fermi's research group,

   a) there was a complete overlap of professional interests
   b) the number of researchers between 15 and 20 in Fermi's inner group was large
   c) the Italian family appears to have been a model for the social relationships that developed
   d) the Italian bureaucracy was the model for the social relationships that developed

8. The success of the Fermi group was partly based on

   a) keeping emotions and intuitions out of the picture
   b) a hierarchical approach
   c) giving authorship to an article to one individual
   d) Fermi's relationship to Corbino

9. One problem which U.S. voluntary organizations presently face is

   a) a declining emphasis on humanitarianism
   b) tax trends that are bad for charity
   c) the influence of coercive organizations
   d) the influence of utilitarian organizations

10. Thurman Arnold's "science of organizations" includes the idea that

a) an organization develops the "personality" of its leader
b) under most conditions, organizations can be radically changed
c) organizations must resolve the gap between ideals and practice
d) organizations disappear once they have fulfilled their usefulness

_____ 11. Coercive organizations

a) are often total institutions
b) are often changed into utilitarian organizations
c) have more "personality" (in Arnold's view) than other organizations
d) are illustrated by the American Legion

_____ 12. Bureaucratic organizations

a) are governmental in almost every case
b) are more dysfunctional for society than functional
c) are more functional for society than dysfunctional
d) may be utilitarian, voluntary or coercive

_____ 13. In bureaucracy, according to Weber's ideal type,

a) administrative acts and rules are recorded in writing
b) administrators can be owners as well
c) there are overlapping spheres of competence for the various positions
d) after a given period, individuals earn exclusive rights to their positions

_____ 14. An ideal type

a) can be observed in reality, but with considerable difficulty
b) represents the aspirations of administrators
c) represents the aspirations of the researcher
d) is an abstract set of characteristics used to highlight key features

_____ 15. Welles' film The Trial illustrates

a) the disadvantages of not having a bureau-

cratic court system
    b) the dysfunctions of voluntary organizations
    c) the dysfunctions of utilitarian organizations
    d) the functions of coercive organizations

_____ 16. Substantive rationality is best illustrated by

    a) the choice of a car based on price alone
    b) the choice of a car based only on price and affordability
    c) the choice of a car based on safety, appearance, repairability, utility, and emotional attachment
    d) none of the above

_____ 17. With regard to formal and informal structures in an organization,

    a) informal structures can be completely eliminated
    b) formal structures can be completely eliminated
    c) informal structures are often not legitimate within the organization
    d) formal structures are generally not legitimate within the organization

_____ 18. In Blau's study of a state employment agency,

    a) application forms were rarely made out
    b) occupational codes were generally used
    c) applicants were selected from application files
    d) counseling was frequently used

_____ 19. Alienation was seen by Karl Marx as

    a) associated with the experience of industrial workers
    b) to be found in voluntary organizations
    c) to be found primarily in coercive organizations
    d) to be found among capitalists as well as workers

_____ 20. Studies of alienation indicate that

    a) it is not a widespread problem
    b) unskilled workers show more boredom than

skilled workers
c) it is more widespread in the printing trades than in the auto industry
d) automation is associated with an overall reduction of alienation

Concept Recognition: Write the concept or term in the blank space next to its definition.

_____ 1. A group deliberately constructed to seek specific goals.

_____ 2. The extent to which accurate calculations can be associated with alternative actions.

_____ 3. Feelings of powerlessness, meaninglessness and social isolation associated with certain social relationships.

_____ 4. An organization with an extensive hierarchy and division of labor governed by explicit rules.

_____ 5. A face-to-face group that is fundamental in forming the personality structure of its members.

_____ 6. The actual pattern of behavior and the values and norms associated with that behavior.

_____ 7. An organization people join because they share the organization's goals.

_____ 8. A set of individuals involved in social relationships who define themselves as a group or are so defined by others.

_____ 9. An organization people join in order to gain important personal benefits.

_____ 10. An organization in which membership is obtained or maintained by force.

True/False: Enter "T" for true or "F" for false for the best answer to the statement.

_____ 1. One source of alienation is the narrowness of organizational goals.

_____ 2. According to Stephen Marks, multiple roles necessarily produce role strain.

_____ 3. An individual may be a member of a group even if he or she is unaware of it.

_____ 4. New Yorkers can be considered a group but not Australians.

_____ 5. People at a given streetcorner waiting for a light to change are a group.

_____ 6. The Fermi group's overlapping interests was an important reason for its success.

_____ 7. Coercive organizations can tolerate very serious conflict between individual and organization.

_____ 8. A coercive organization is similar to a total institution.

_____ 9. Organizations, according to Thurman Arnold, develop a personality or character of their own.

_____10. Weber's "ideal type" for bureaucracy referred to its informal structure.

Concept Definition: Write the definition of the concept or term appearing on the left in the blank space next to it.

1. degredation ceremony _____

_____

2. informal structure _____

_____

3. aggregate _____

_____

4. role strain _____

_____

5. formal structure _____

6.　ideal type _____

7.　primary group _____

8.　substantive rationality _____

9.　secondary group _____

10. alienation _____

ANSWERS

Self Quiz

1.	c	6.	b	11.	a	16.	c
2.	a	7.	c	12.	d	17.	c
3.	d	8.	d	13.	a	18.	a
4.	d	9.	b	14.	d	19.	a
5.	b	10.	c	15.	a	20.	b

Concept Recognition

1.　organization
2.　formal rationality
3.　alienation
4.　bureaucracy
5.　primary group

6.　informal structure
7.　voluntary organization
8.　group
9.　utilitarian organization
10.　coercive organization

True-False

1.	T	6.	T
2.	F	7.	T
3.	T	8.	T
4.	F	9.	T
5.	F	10.	F

Concept Definition

See Glossary in back of this booklet

The Community

15

OVERVIEW

Communities in preindustrial, industrial and postindustrial societies differ from one another. For example, industrial (as distinct from preindustrial) cities
are characterized by continuing growth and emphasize
a scientifically-based technology as well as bureaucracy.
Trends in postindustrial cities emphasize services (such
as education, recreation, medical care), movement to the
suburbs, and then to the suburbs of those suburbs. The
city has been portrayed by many--including sociologists--
as a kind of Sodom or Gemorrah, in contrast to the rural
Garden of Eden. Attitudes of people moving to cities--
such as migrants to Skopje, Yugoslavia--testify to the
positive features of the city. City planning has affected
the nature of cities in many ways, and has als resulted
in controversies. For example, urban renewal procedures have been condemned by many for destroying neigh-
borhoods.

SYNOPSIS

15.1 The Nature of the Community

  a Definitions

     A community is a group, as distinct from a piece

175

of territory, but it is also a group occupying a given territorial area. Whereas an organization is deliberately constructed around particular goals, a community is not deliberately constructed (in general). Moreover, the people in a community share goals that are sufficiently wide-ranging so that they are able to live wholly within the community.

b   Stages of Industrialization

Communities vary greatly depending on the stage of industrialization of the society in which they are located. Preindustrial cities are located in societies in which the vast majority of the people are involved in agriculture. Industrial societies, by contrast, have a substantial proportion of people involved in the production of goods. And post-industrial societies experience a decreasing percentage in manufacturing, a stabilized low percentage in agriculture, and an increasing percentage in services.

15.2   The Community in Preindustrial, Industrial and Post-industrial Society

a   Origins of the Preindustrial City

Sjoberg sees three factors necessary for the rise of the preindustrial city: a favorable physical environment, advanced technology, and well-developed social structures. The latter is illustrated by the emergence of a very small group of ruling warriors and priests who coordinated the exchange and distribution of goods and services.

b   Rise of the Industrial City

These same factors are also involved in the development of the industrial city. Its technology, by contrast, is based on scientific knowledge and takes on the scientific ideal of progress. And that idea constitutes a partial explanation for the continuing growth of the industrial city, by contrast with the cycles of growth and decline of preindustrial cities.

c   Urbanization

Urbanization does not simply refer to the size of cities: it has to do with an increasing proportion of an entire society that is concentrated within small territorial areas. A society is not, then, urbanizing if there is no shift away from the countryside, as illustrated by a decrease in the proportion of the population working on the farm. Some of the advantages of life in the city--which helps to explain migration to the city--are illustrated by a study of migrants to Skopje, Yugoslavia. They mention, for example, a higher standard of living, expanded cultural and intellectual opportunities, and improved occupational opportunities.

d   Growth of Suburbs and the Metropolis

During this past century suburbs have grown enormously in the U.S. Suburbs, along with central cities and satellite cities (small manufacturing cities tending to be older than the residential suburbs), make up a given metropolitan area. Myths about the uniformity and political conservativeness to be found in the suburbs, as portrayed by novels such as Keats' The Crack in the Picture Window, are disputed by present-day researchers. Suburbs include--in addition to middle-income residential suburbs--working-class suburbs, old rural towns engulfed by migrants, and traditional upper-class suburbs.

e   Rise of the Megalopolis

Bigger even than the metropolitan area is the megalopolis: a region including several large cities and their surrounding areas. These are illustrated by the Northeastern seabord of the U.S. from south of Washington to Boston, and by the Dallas-San Antonio-Houston region in Texas. There are thirteen such areas in the U.S., designated by the Census Bureau as Standard Consolidated Areas.

f   Recent Trends in the Suburbs

Recently there is a migration trend from metropolitan areas to non-metropolitan counties adjacent to those areas. This trend, coupled with the continuing migration from central cities to suburbs within metropolitan areas, means a shift of the population to less densely populated areas. Another change is toward increasing interest in preserving the natural environment.

15.3 Images of the City

a Widespread Images

From the bible we have images of the evil city
(Sod-m and Gemorrah) as well as of the rural para-
dise (the Garden of Eden). Such images are encouraged within much of popular culture, as illustrated by the glorification of the American West.
In a study of a small town in upstate New York, the
big city is seen by residents as a dog-eat-dog
environment, full of crime, atheism and evil ways,
in contrast to small-town or rural virtues. The
recency of our urbanization process is a partial
explanation for these images.

b Early Sociological Images

Louis Wirth's "Urbanism as a Way of Life" continues
a tradition, encouraged by Tonnies' view of the
distinction between gemeinschaft and gesellschaft,
of the city as encouraging impersonal and superficial human contact. Durkheim, who was optimistic
about industrial life in his Division of Labor with
its concept of organic solidarity, emphasized the
importance of close personal relationships in his
Suicide. Simmel's views are mixed.

c A Contemporary Sociological Image

Warren distinguishes between vertical and horizontal patterns within the community. In the former,
as illustrated by the chain store, elements within
the community are subservient to external hierarchies, and this may be associated with the "eclipse
of community." In the latter, as illustrated by
relationships among schools, churches and voluntary
organizations within the community (such as a United
Fund drive), social structures within the community
form relationships. The decline of the local political machine in favor of a shift to state or national political centers illustrates a change from
the horizontal to the vertical pattern.

15.4 City Planning

a The Garden City

El Armana (Near East, 1358 B.C.), Washington,D.C.,
New Delhi and Brazilia exemplify cities that have

been planned. Ebenezer Howard developed his "Garden City" concept in 1898 as a means for stemming migration to London and repopulating the countryside. He proposed the building of new communities with populations under thirty thousand, surrounded by a belt of agriculture, and with the scheme to be preserved through the permanent control of a public authority. Such towns as Stevenage and Harlow (Britain) as well as Reston and Columbia (U.S.) were influenced by the Garden City concept.

b   Focus on Services

A trend within postindustrial new towns is to plan certain of them around particular services, such as a "Disney-World" amusement center, a shopping center or a university.

c   Controversies over City Planning

Le Corbusier's "Radiant City" idea (skyscrapers within a park) departs radically from the Garden City idea and, thus, illustrates controversies within city-planning groups. Jane Jacobs objects to the mechanization involved in Radiant City as well as the isolation resulting from the rectangular superblock. She sees Boston's Italian-American North End--with its small and irregular streets, old houses, mixture of establishments and enormous vitality--as illustrating what cities have to offer. Herbert Gans, in his study of urban renewal in Boston's West End, documented the destruction of that neighborhood through the wholesale removal of its residents. However, there are functions as well as dysfunctions associated with urban renewal, as in other approaches to city planning. Such an approach, moreover, can be planned so as to involve the removal of very few existing residences and commercial establishments.

SELF-QUIZ

Multiple Choice: In the space provided, enter the letter
of the answer that best completes the question.

_____ 1. A community is

        a) a group
        b) a territorial area
        c) an area with certain characteristics (such
           as high population density)
        d) the product of urbanization

_____ 2. A community-like group is best illustrated by

        a) an old-age home
        b) a prison
        c) a mental hospital
        d) a family

_____ 3. Postindustrial and industrial societies are
           related in that

        a) both involve a declining proportion in
           agriculture
        b) both involve an increasing percentage in
           services
        c) both involve a decreasing percentage in
           manufacturing
        d) all of the above

_____ 4. Technology is best illustrated by

        a) the laws of mechanics
        b) the division of labor in society
        c) procedures for establishing a bureaucracy
        d) procedures for the domestication of wheat

_____ 5. Urbanization refers to

        a) the growth of communities
        b) the depopulation of the countryside
        c) the above trends in society as a whole
        d) the existence of cities over 2 million in
           size

_____ 6. Concerning migration to Skopje, Yugoslavia,

        a) migrants generally did not want to move but
           were forced to

180

b) migrants saw many advantages to life in Skopje
c) migrants were unhappy about the political system
d) migrants were unhappy about unemployment

_____ 7. Wethersfield, a housing subdivision in the Boston area,

a) has become more heterogeneous over the years
b) has incorporated as a town
c) is based on Garden City principles
d) is based on Radiant City principles

_____ 8. A Standard Consolidated Area

a) is a megalopolis
b) is illustrated by Chicago
c) is a metropolis
d) is a huge suburban belt surrounded by forests

_____ 9. According to the 1970 census of the U.S. population,

a) most people live in suburbs
b) most people live in central cities
c) most people live in nonmetropolitan areas
d) most people live in metropolitan areas

_____ 10. Between 1970 and 1974, in the U.S., there is a new migration from

a) nonmetropolitan to metropolitan areas
b) metropolitan to nonmetropolitan areas
c) suburbs to central cities
d) nonmetropolitan areas to central cities

_____ 11. Widespread popular images of the city and rural life in the U.S. tend to emphasize

a) positive features of both cities and rural life
b) negative features of both cities and rural life
c) negative features of cities and positive features of rural life
d) positive features of cities and negative features of rural life

181

12. Vidich and Bensman portrayed Springdalers attitudes about life in the big city as including this idea:

a) intellectual stimulation in the city
b) industrial workers are overpaid and their leaders are troublemakers
c) the city has greater possibilities for theatre and concerts
d) the city offers more chances for a wider circle of friends

13. Which of these sociologists did not generally view the city in an unfavorable light:

a) Tonnies
b) Wirth
c) Park
d) Durkheim

14. The vertical pattern of a community is best illustrated by

a) a community United Fund drive
b) a federal grant for the building of a new town
c) a meeting between the Parent Teachers Assoc. and other voluntary groups in the community
d) a meeting among businessmen within the community

15. The power of the local political machine in the U.S.

a) is increasing once again
b) illustrates the vertical pattern
c) has decreased
d) is opposed by the Radiant City idea

16. Planned cities include

a) Chicago
b) Los Angeles
c) Washington D.C.
d) New York

17. Part of the Garden City idea is that

a) changes in land use are to be under the permanent control of a public authority

b) industry is to be located in the center of the city
c) the size is to be limited to 100,000
d) the community is to be surrounded by a dense forest

_____ 18. Examples of the Garden City approach include

a) Stockholm
b) Oslo
c) Moscow
d) Stevenage

_____ 19. The Radiant City idea is best illustrated by

a) the street plan for New Orleans
b) the highway system surrounding Houston
c) some high-rise apartment houses in New York
d) Boston's North End

_____ 20. Urban renewal

a) requires the tearing down of almost all existing dwellings
b) has frequently destroyed neighborhood relationships
c) is almost completely dysfunctional
d) is almost completely functional

Concept Recognition: Write the concept or term in the blank space next to its definition.

_____ 1. Small manufacturing cities within a metropolitan area, tending to be older than the residential suburbs.

_____ 2. Any group that emerges without having been deliberately constructed to seek specific goals.

_____ 3. The body of available methods for shaping the physical environment.

_____ 4. A community's organized relations to social structures outside of its boundaries.

_____ 5. A region consisting of several large cities and their surrounding areas that make up a single urban complex.

183

_____ 6. A rise in the proportion of the total population of a society that is concentrated within relatively small territorial areas.

_____ 7. A society in which the vast majority of the population is engaged in agriculture.

_____ 8. A community surrounded by a belt of agriculture with a maximum population of thirty thousand people.

_____ 9. Urban areas which include one or more central cities, suburban areas, and satellite cities.

_____10. A society in which the percentage of those employed in agriculture stabilizes at a very low level, with a continuing decrease of the percentage in manufacturing and increase of the percentage in services.

True/False: Enter "T" for true or "F" for false for the best answer to the statement.

_____ 1. Technology is illustrated by a system of navigable rivers.

_____ 2. Scientific knowledge is a major basis for the continuing growth of the industrial city.

_____ 3. Urbanization in the U.S.S.R. exceeds that in England.

_____ 4. Migration to Skopje was largely based on the attractions offered by the city.

_____ 5. A small, new, nonmanufacturing city located just beyond a metropolis is called a Standard Metropolitan City.

_____ 6. According to recent research, informal visiting and friendship patterns are no longer found in suburbs.

_____ 7. There is only one Standard Consolidated Area, as yet, in the U.S.: the Northeastern Seabord from Washington to Boston.

_____ 8.   The biblical description of the Garden of Eden
             presents a positive image of rural life.

_____ 9.   Springdalers, according to Vidich and Bensman,
             view life in Springdale as encouraging honesty
             and a wholesome family experience.

_____10.   According to Georg Simmel, the city-dweller
             tends to gain a higher degree of consciousness
             resulting from the city's tempo and diversity.

Concept Definition: Write the definition of the concept
or term appearing on the left in the blank space next to
it.

1. community social profile _____

_____

2. urbanization _____

_____

3. community _____

_____

4. Standard Metropolitan Statistical Area _____

_____

5. horizontal pattern of a community _____

_____

6. Radiant City _____

_____

7. industrial society _____

_____

8. preindustrial society _____

_____

9. community-like group _____

_____

10. postindustrial city _____

_____

ANSWERS

Self Quiz

1.	a	6.	b	11.	c	16.	c
2.	d	7.	a	12.	b	17.	a
3.	b	8.	a	13.	d	18.	d
4.	d	9.	d	14.	b	19.	c
5.	c	10.	b	15.	c	20.	b

Concept Recognition

1. satellite cities
2. community-like group
3. technology
4. vertical pattern of a
   community
5. magalopolis

6. urbanization
7. preindustrial society
8. Garden City
9. metropolitan areas
10. postindustrial society

True-False

1.	F	6.	F
2.	T	7.	F
3.	F	8.	T
4.	T	9.	T
5.	F	10.	T

Concept Definition

See Glossary in back of this booklet

Society
16

OVERVIEW

Society should not be confused with the state, which
is a bureaucratic organization with a monopoly over the
legitimate use of force or violence. The nature and
power of the state is illustrated from popular culture
by the failure of world leaders, along with Spiderman,
to get rid of Dr. Doom, the ruler of a sovereign state.
Countercultures of different types have developed in
postindustrial societies. They are subcultures and,
thus, not totally opposed to dominant norms and values.
In the U.S. the student counterculture which developed
in the 1960s, with its emphasis on emotional expression,
appears to be losing its expressive emphasis. Perhaps
this is due in part to its failure to come to terms with
such features of society as bureaucracy.

SYNOPSIS

16.1 Types of Societies

  a State and Society

     A state is an organization. As such, it is delib-
     erately constructed to seek particular goals. A
     society, by contrast, is a community-like group.
     By distinguishing between the two we are able to

insight into situations in which state and society
are opposed, as illlustrated by the evil ways of
Dr. Doom, who is the head of a state. The conflict
between state and society is further illustrated
by the conflict within the U.S. over the war in
Vietnam. An illustration of a situation in which
state and society are in greater harmony comes
from the film <u>Ivan the Terrible</u>. Ivan's rise to
the position of the first Czar of Russia is portrayed as furthering the interests of society as
a whole, as distinct from the narrow feudal interests of the Oprichniks.

b   Preindustrial and Industrial Societies

Every preindustrial society differs from every
other one, and the same is true for industrial as
well as for postindustrial societies. Yet it is
still possible to characterize preindustrial societies in general, although we should remain aware
of the limitations of any such profile. In general,
preindustrial societies have these characteristics:
(1) slow or variable population growth, with few
cities over 100,000; (2) rule by a small political
and religious elite; (3) a rigid stratification
system (little upward mobility); (4) arranged marriages; (5) dominance of women by men and the young
by the old; (6) a simple technology based on human
and animal power; (7) organizations with rigid
hierarchies and centralization of societal power
within a single leader; and (8) regulation of most
areas of life by religious leaders who tend to think
in absolute terms.

An industrial society, by contrast, may be characterized by: (1) population growth; (2) patterns
of upward mobility and status inconsistency; (3)
individual choice of marriage partner; (4) sex
roles which allow for greater diversity in behavior;
(5) economies oriented to mass production and an
intricate division of labor; (6) standardization
of prices, currency, and weights and measures; (7)
large-scale bureaucracies; (8) a high degree of
formal education; and (9) a scientific tradition
that de-emphasizes absolutist modes of thought.

c   Some Aspects of Postindustrial Society

As an industrial society transforms into a postindustrial one, its occupational force continues

188

to alter its directions. Service organizations--
producing intangible products (such as trade,
finance, transport, health, education, and government)--become more prominent. The proportion of
people engaged in factory work continues to decline. Only a very small proportion of the work
force remains on the farm.

The approach to production is also changed in a
postindustrial society. Bell, for example, points
to a greater concern with the quality of life, as
illustrated by health, education, recreation, and
the arts. Schumacher points to increasing concern
over the depletion of irreplaceable natural resources. Galbraith refers to a new struggle re-
placing the class struggle between employers and
unions: that between the individual and the organization. International relations are crucial in
the postindustrial society. Rubinson's study of
international stratification suggests the importance of economic factors. Some states continue
to dominate others by penetrating them economically
as well as becoming decreasingly dependent on them.
Also, states at the top of the stratification system can protect themselves through trade and tar-
iff policies and force out foreign investors when
desirable. Further, strong states, as distinct
from weak ones, can afford a more equalitarian
distribution of income within their boundaries.

16.2 Culture and Counterculture

a The Nature of Counterculture

A counterculture is a subculture and, thus, is part
of culture. In addition, elements of a counterculture are opposed to elements of the culture prevailing in society as a whole. And there are different kinds of countercultures in different places
and periods of time. Cox's study of religious
groups in the Harvard Square area illustrates the
nature of present-day counterculture in the U.S.
Groups such as the Sufi dancers and the followers
of Zen are deeply concerned with seeking simple
human friendship, immediacy of experience, and some
source of authority. These are ideals or values
similar to those in American society as a whole.
Points of opposition include a rejection of the
abstract intellect and the Western scientific tradition.

Reich's Greening of America is a much-discussed
statement of the nature of American student counterculture, especially as it existed in the late 1960s.
He centers on the power of subcultural changes--
such as styles in clothes, music, drugs and thought--
to produce profound cultural and societal changes.
Reviewers have generally been critical, referring
to the negative features of American counterculture
and Reich's naive ideas about how easy it is to
change society.

Revel's view of cultural change portrays the U.S.
as the most revolutionary country in the world. He
sees many different kinds of changes as closely
related: the student movement, the black revolt,
women's liberation, the growing demand for equality,
and the concern for the natural environment.

b Culture and Counterculture in Magazines and Newspapers

In a quantitative study of counterculture in the
U.S., Canada and Great Britain, Spates compares
the values expressed in newspapers and magazines
in the late 1950s with those of the early 1970s.
He finds an increasing movement of counterculture
toward the dominant culture. For example, the
instrumental orientation (focus on actions necessary to achieve future goals) has been emphasized
to a greater extent within counterculture. Also,
counterculture shifted to a much-reduced emphasis
on an expressive orientation (a focus on the immediate gratification of desires). Yinger, who coined
the term "counterculture," concludes that cultural
change can only proceed a certain distance without
changes in social relationships along with changes
in personality or character. Political changes by
themselves do not necessarily result in fundamental
societal changes. This is illustrated by the saying,
"Radicals fight the revolution; conservatives write
the constitution."

c Bureaucratic Settings and the Persistence of Counterculture

Zucker, by means of an experiment that measured conformity to the statements of confederates in an
ambiguous situation, was able to assess the influence of bureaucratic settings in attaining such conformity. She found that when a setting was changed

190

from an informal to a formal one, conformity increased. Further, when the formal setting became more bureaucratic, conformity increased still further. And such conformity could be passed on from one set of subjects to the next over many "generations" of subjects. From this, we might infer the importance of the norms and values prevailing in bureaucracies in determining the future of American counterculture.

Multiple Choice: In the space provided, enter the letter of the answer that best completes the question.

_____ 1. In the excerpt on Spiderman and Dr. Doom, the world's leaders are reluctant to deal harshly with Dr. Doom because

    a) he is the ruler of a sovereign state
    b) he genuinely is pushing for the interests of his society
    c) Spiderman will take care of Dr. Doom himself
    d) they are trying to be fair to their own people

_____ 2. According to Napoleon, his military success in his Spanish campaign was based on moral factors to what extent:

    a) one quarter
    b) half
    c) three-quarters
    d) moral considerations were not a significant factor

_____ 3. The French defeat of the English in the fifteenth century, as portrayed in Shaw's Saint Joan, best illustrates

    a) the conflict between the desires of a government and the desires of its people
    b) the convergence or harmony between the desires of a government and the desires of its people
    c) the difficulties of getting rid of a ruler once he is in power
    d) the superficiality of political changes

_____ 4. The film, Ivan the Terrible, which portrays the rise of Russia's first Czar, best illustrates

    a) the conflict between the desires of a government and the desires of its people
    b) the convergence or harmony between the desires of a government and the desires of its people
    c) the difficulties of getting rid of a ruler once he is in power

d) the superficiality of political changes

_____ 5. Preindustrial societies may be generally characterized by

a) avoidance of economic activity
b) a rural elite
c) rule by an educational and familistic elite
d) a simple division of labor

_____ 6. Industrial societies may be generally characterized by

a) the centralization of authority within a
single sovereign leader
b) an absolutist mode of thought
c) dominance of women by men in the family
d) continuing population growth

_____ 7. In Small Is Beautiful, Schumacher argues that

a) the using up of irreplaceable resources is
not a serious problem
b) pollution is not a serious problem
c) production tends to separate the worker
from meaningful relationships with others
d) the fundamental problems of production have
been solved

_____ 8. Daniel Bell views the postindustrial society
as

a) less concerned with quantity than the quality
b) concerned with the tangible products of production
c) involved in increasing centralization
d) involved in a continuing struggle between
owners and workers

_____ 9. Galbraith, in his The Affluent Society, pre-
sents the idea that

a) our economic thought is no longer rooted
in poverty and inequality
b) our religious thought is no longer rooted
in poverty and inequality
c) we are on the road to shorter hours of work
and pleasanter working conditions
d) our desires for affluence must be balanced
by a realistic view of continuing--and per-

haps increasing--scarcity

_____ 10. Rubinson, in his study of international stratification, points out that

a) the U.S. is in the "First World"
b) the developing nations are in the "Third
World"
c) international strength is based on armies
and military hardware more than economic
factors
d) greater income inequality exists in nations
at a lower level within the international
stratification system

_____ 11. Counterculture and culture are related in that

a) both are aspects of a subculture
b) a culture is a type of counterculture
c) both focus on social relationships
d) both focus on norms and values

_____ 12. Cox found, in his study of religious groups
in Harvard Square, that those involved were
seeking

a) simple human friendship
b) immediacy of experience
c) both of the above
d) neither a) nor b)

_____ 13. Reich, in Greening of America, expresses the
idea that

a) important aspects of the youth rebellion
are profoundly anti-democratic
b) counterculture is coming to all people in
America
c) there is profound anti-intellectualism within the new generation
d) the National Guard and the armed forces are
still quite powerful

_____ 14. Revel's approach to cultural change includes
the idea that

a) a cultural revolution will occur first in
the U.S.
b) the black revolt is not part of America's
cultural revolution

c) America's youth are very far along on the path to cultural revolution
d) the feminist attack on male domination is not part of America's cultural revolution

_____ 15. Spates' study of counterculture and dominant culture revealed that

a) dominant culture magazines have shifted in a political direction
b) dominant culture magazines have become more expressive
c) dominant culture magazines have become more instrumental
d) dominant culture magazines have become more religious

_____ 16. Yinger's analysis of cultural change indicates that

a) change in counterculture can easily fail to yield widespread cultural change
b) political changes are generally highly effective in producing widespread cultural change
c) cultural change need not be combined with changes in social relationships to produce deep societal change
d) cultural change need not be combined with character change to produce deep societal change

_____ 17. The Little Prince best illustrates the idea that

a) state rulers have enormous power
b) cultural change can occur very rapidly
c) society holds far more power than any national ruler
d) counterculture is a part of culture

_____ 18. In Zucker's experiment, conformity was greatest in

a) an informal setting
b) a bureaucratic setting
c) a formal setting
d) a primary-group setting

_____ 19. In Zucker's experiment, changes that occurred
persisted most in

   a) an informal setting
   b) a bureaucratic setting
   c) a formal setting
   d) a primary-group setting

_____ 20. The saying, "Radicals fight the revolution;
conservatives write the constitution," implies
(according to the text) that

   a) radical change in society can easily occur
   b) cultural change can easily fail to yield
      political change
   c) it is difficult to create persisting change
      in society as a whole
   d) conservatives are, in a sense, more radical
      than radicals

Concept Recognition: Write the concept or term in the
blank space next to its definition.

_____ 1. An organization with a monopoly
on the legitimate use of violence within a society.

_____ 2. A subculture focused on opposition to the culture prevailing in society as a
whole.

_____ 3. An emphasis on immediate gratification of desires rather than making progress
toward future goals.

_____ 4. A system of expectations and
goals widely shared within a subgroup of society.

_____ 5. A group broad enough to include
all subgroups having a basis in the same culture.

_____ 6. An organization producing intangible products.

_____ 7. A focus on attaining some future
goal and an action as a means for attaining it.

True/False: Enter "T" for true or "F" for false for the
best answer to the statement.

_____ 1. Power is not based on legitimacy.

_____ 2. Rulers of states, according to the Spiderman illustration, are generally seen as morally legitimate.

_____ 3. A preindustrial society generally have an out-caste group, such as slaves or foreigners.

_____ 4. An industrial society generally is character-ized by almost universal patterns of status consistency.

_____ 5. Blue-collar workers tend to be a growing occu-pational group in a postindustrial society.

_____ 6. According to Rubinson, the gap is closing between rich and poor nations.

_____ 7. A counterculture is not a subculture.

_____ 8. Some critics of Reich's Greening of America say his presentation was extremely one-sided.

_____ 9. Revel believes that socialist politics may produce dogma and actually slow down a cultural revolution.

_____10. Spates' analysis indicates that American counter-culture is moving in the direction of the dom-inant culture rather than the reverse.

Concept Definition: Write the definition of the concept or term appearing on the left in the blank space next to it.

1. service organization _____

_____

2. society _____

_____

3. instrumental orientation _____

_____

4. state _____

5.   subculture _____

_____

6.   expressive orientation _____

_____

7.   counterculture _____

_____

ANSWERS

Self Quiz

1.	a	6.	d	11.	d	16.	a
2.	c	7.	c	12.	c	17.	c
3.	b	8.	a	13.	b	18.	b
4.	b	9.	c	14.	a	19.	b
5.	d	10.	d	15.	a	20.	c

Concept Recognition

1.   state
2.   counterculture
3.   expressive orientation
4.   subculture

5.   society
6.   service organization
7.   instrumental orientation

True-False

1.	F	6.	F
2.	T	7.	F
3.	T	8.	T
4.	F	9.	T
5.	F	10.	T

Concept Definition

See Glossary in back of this booklet

Population

17

OVERVIEW

Biological evolution has resulted--in <u>Homo sapiens</u>--
in organisms with exceptional intelligence and capacities
for developing language, giving mankind unusual capacities for adaptation. But can we learn to deal with problems of overpopulation? In 1798 Thomas Malthus asserted
his principle of exponential population growth, yet it
appears that no such tendency is rooted in human phys-
iology. The demographic transition, which is the lower-
ing of birth and death rates that accompanies industrialization, illustrate a departure from this principle.
Currently, there is debate within sociology over the
seriousness of the problem of overpopulation.

SYNOPSIS

17.1 <u>Biological Structure and Human Limitations</u>

a Biological Structures

A biological structure is bounded, that is, it is
located in space and time, and not simply a mental
construction. Also, it is a relatively open system
in that it interacts to a fair extent with its
environment. And it has the capacity to reproduce
itself.

b   Biological Evolution

Biological evolution is a process of change, occurring from one generation to the next, in the biological structure of organisms. The key unit involved is the gene, which largely controls an organism's biological structure. Genes can undergo
mutation or change. The vast majority of mutations
decrease the biological adaptation of the organism
(its ability to adjust to the environment), but
some mutations improve the organism's adaptation.
Thus, over vast numbers of years, biological evolution can result in organisms that are very well
adapted to the environment.

The adaptation of the human being can proceed in
other ways than biological adaptation. Learning
is a very important process in our species, and
it takes place in an infinitesimal time period
relative to the slowness of biological adaptation.
Learning is a relatively permanent change in behavior resulting from experience. Our intelligence
or capacity for learning is high, partly due to
our large brain and partly to our capacity to develop speech and language. Learning is made possible by the nature of our biological structure.
As a result, humans do not have to depend on genetic mutation to improve their adaptation to the
environment. But learning is not inevitable: we
have the capacity to learn, but how far we develop
ourselves is up to us.

17.2 Population Characteristics

a   Birth and Death Rates

Demographers, who study human populations, are
particularly interested in those factors that
affect population size. Thus, birth and death
rates are of special concern. They are ratios of
births and deaths to the total size of the population, and thus they make it easy to compare tendencies toward population growth or decay in areas
with different populations. The natural increase
rate, obtained by subtracting the death rate from
the birth rate, is a single measure of the tendency
toward growth. In the U.S., a great deal of information about population characteristics is collected
by the U.S. Census every ten years. Birth and death
rates vary greatly in different countries.

b   Population Density

Population density is population size per unit area.
The highest densities in the world are to be found
in Japan, India, Bangladesh, the Federal Republic
of Germany, the United Kingdom, Italy and the Philippines. Nations with the lowest densities are
the U.S.S.R., the U.S., Brazil, Mexico and Egypt.
Information about density must be combined with
other information to shed light on important questions. For example, the People's Republic of China
is not one of the densest nations in the world. Yet
that nation affects the size of the world's population more than other nations because its present
population is close to 850 million.

c   Population Projections

Although demographers cannot predict the size of
future populations, they can make population projections. These give the size of future populations under certain assumptions. For example, if
the completed fertility rate (average number of
births per woman for her entire life) is 2.0, then
a population will tend to remain stable. This stability will occur on the assumption that there is
no net immigration and that the death rate is low.
By contrast, a cfr of 2.7 along with an annual net
immigration of 400,000 will result in a U.S. population of 500 million by the year 2050.

d   Immigration

Between 1970 and 1975 immigration to the U.S. aver-
aged 400,000 per year. Recently, immigration has
come primarily from Spanish-speaking areas (Mexico,
the Philippines, and Cuba). Movement from Puerto
Rico to the mainland is called migration, since
Puerto Rico is part of the U.S. There were great
waves of immigration to the U.S. at the turn of
this century and for several decades afterward,
with New York and Boston being the major points of
entry.

17.3 Trends in Population Size

a   Thomas Malthus: Exponential Population Growth?

In 1798 Malthus published his influential Essay on
the Principle of Population. The principle is that

201

population will increase geometrically (doubling every twenty-five years), whereas food supply can at best increase arithmetically. Thus, "positive" checks to population growth, such as high death rates and illness, will tend to occur in the long run without "preventative" checks. The latter were, for Malthus, primarily the abstinence from sexual relationships. Today, however, artificial birth control procedures would be so classified.

The world's population has indeed grown rapidly, but it has not grown exponentially. For example, the U.S. population increased from 39.8 million in 1870 to 203.2 million in 1970. Four doublings during this hundred-year period would, by contrast, have produced a total of 636.8 million. And during this period, there was heavy immigration to the U.S. In the world generally, population is increasing rapidly in some areas (notably Latin America and Africa) but only slowly in other areas (Japan and Europe).

b   The Demographic Transition

Major changes in birth and death rates are associated with the industrial revolution. The demographic transition refers to the change from high to low birth and death rates. During an intermediate stage within this transition, birth rates are high while death rates are low, producing rapid population growth. Present-day industrialized nations have passed through this transition. However, if nonindustrialized nations in Latin America, Africa and Asia do the same, serious overpopulation problems might result. This would occur because of the intermediate stage of that transition, coupling with the large population base that many nonindustrialized nations start with. Presently, death rates in Latin America and many other nonindustrialized areas throughout the world are falling sharply while birth rates remain high.

c   Overpopulation and Governmental Policies

The issue of overpopulation is a controversial one. For example, the biologist Ehrlich maintains that Americans must lower their birth rate or face a drastic rise in their death rate. He also believes that schemes for vastly increasing food supply are unrealistic, and that family planning is almost a

202

complete failure in India and hasn't worked that
well in Japan. By contrast, the sociologist Bogue
believes that the world population crisis will be
a thing of the past in the next century. Bogue
further believes that the rate of population growth
"will slacken with each passing year," and that
"the world is on the threshold of a 'contraceptive
adoptive explosion.'"

SELF-QUIZ

Multiple Choice: In the space provided, enter the letter
of the answer that best completes the question.

_____ 1. A biological structure, an open system and a
bounded system are related in that

   a) a tree illustrates all of them
   b) a crystal illustrates all of them
   c) the solar system illustrates all of them
   d) the milky way galaxy illustrates all of
      them

_____ 2. A closed system

   a) has the capacity to reproduce itself
   b) does not exist in the universe
   c) is illustrated by any biological structure
   d) is best illustrated by a rock

_____ 3. Biological evolution and biological adaptation
are related in that

   a) both refer to improved biological adaptation
   b) both involve mutations
   c) both tend to occur within a single genera-
      tion
   d) both occur in most but not all species

_____ 4. Mutations and learning are related in that

   a) both refer to changes in behavior
   b) both refer to changes in biological struc-
      ture
   c) both may enable the organisms to improve
      its adaptation
   d) both take place generally within a single
      generation

_____ 5. Intelligence, language, learning, and large
brain size are related in that

   a) all are found to a great extent in human
      beings
   b) all are the result in large measure of a
      given biological structure
   c) both of the above
   d) neither of the above

_____ 6. Demography does not generally include

   a) the study of population characteristics
   b) the study of population changes and the analysis of reasons for those changes
   c) estimates of population trends in the future
   d) conducting family planning clinics

_____ 7. The current birth rate for the U.S. is approximately

   a) 95
   b) 60
   c) 30
   d) 15

_____ 8. The current rate of natural increase for the U.S. is approximately

   a) 65
   b) 20
   c) 5
   d) 0

_____ 9. The country with the highest birth rate (among the following) is

   a) Italy
   b) U.S.S.R.
   c) Nigeria
   d) Japan

_____ 10. The country among the following with the greatest population density is

   a) Japan
   b) Mexico
   c) Nigeria
   d) Turkey

_____ 11. Mainland China affects world population trends so much because

   a) her rate of natural increase is almost the highest in the world
   b) her population is the largest in the world
   c) her birth rate is almost the highest in the world
   d) her death rate is almost the lowest in the

world

_____ 12. Which completed fertility rate (assuming a
low death rate and no net immigration) will
tend to keep the population of China stable:

a) 4.0
b) 3.0
c) 2.0
d) 1.0

_____ 13. Which completed fertility rate (assuming a
low death rate and no net immigration) will
tend to keep the population of the U.S. stable:

a) 4.0
b) 3.0
c) 2.0
d) 1.0

_____ 14. Between 1970 and 1975 immigration to the U.S.
has come primarily from

a) Italy
b) the Balkans
c) Spain and Portugal
d) Mexico and the Philippines

_____ 15. Thomas Malthus maintained that

a) preventative checks on population are possible and desirable
b) positive checks on population are more
desirable than preventative checks
c) both preventative and positive checks on
the population should be employed by governmental officials
d) population inevitably increases geometrically,
and no checks will be able to prevent this

_____ 16. Malthus believed that

a) food supply can at best increase arithmetically
b) population can at most increase arithmetically
c) food supply tends to increase geometrically
d) the population tends to triple every ten
years unless checked

_____ 17. The population of the U.S., between 1870 and 1970,

    a) has increased geometrically
    b) has increased as a result of large-scale immigration as well as through natural increases
    c) has increased geometrically
    d) has increased both arithmetically and geo-metrically

_____ 18. Between 1950 and 1975, the world population

    a) has increased geometrically
    b) has increased by about 1 1/2 billion (from 2 1/2 to 4 billion)
    c) has increased by about 3 billion (from 3 to 6 billion)
    d) has tripled (from 2 to 6 billion)

_____ 19. In the second or early industrial stage of the demographic transition,

    a) both birth and death rates fall dramatically
    b) birth and death rates rise moderately, then both fall
    c) birth rates fall, but death rates remain relatively stable
    d) death rates fall, but birth rates remain relatively stable

_____ 20. At the present time, birth rates in Latin America

    a) are remaining very high or else falling very slightly
    b) are increasing slightly (in general)
    c) are generally very close to death rates
    d) are falling faster than death rates

Concept Recognition: Write the concept or term in the blank space next to its definition.

_____ 1. A bounded and relatively open system with the capacity to reproduce itself.

_____ 2. The average number of births per woman throughout her lifetime.

_____ 3. Birth rate minus death rate.

_____ 4. The change from high to low
birth and death rates accompanying industrialization.

_____ 5.   registered deaths

                                _____ x 1,000

          midyear population

_____ 6. A series of terms in which each
term is a constant multiple of the immediately preceding term.

_____ 7. The process of change in the
biological structure of organisms from generation
to generation.

_____ 8. A fundamental hereditary unit
in all organisms that influences biological structures and is capable of mutation or change.

_____ 9. A complete count of a population.

_____ 10. Biological changes which improve the ability of organisms to adjust to the
environment or to alter the environment so that
it adjusts to themselves.

True/False: Enter "T" for true or "F" for false for the
best answer to the statement.

_____ 1. A tree and a planet are both closed systems.

_____ 2. Biological evolution necessarily involves
       genetic changes.

_____ 3. The intelligence of human beings is not based
       on language.

_____ 4. Population projections are fairly accurate
       predictions of the size of the population that
       will actually occur in the future.

_____ 5. Birth and death rates tend to change in oppo-
       site directions.

_____ 6.   It is possible for a probability sample survey
            to be more accurate than a complete census.

_____ 7.   A high population density necessarily implies
            a high birth rate.

_____ 8.   A low natural increase rate necessarily im-
            plies a low rate of population growth.

_____ 9.   At present, the rate of growth in the world's
            population is not exponential.

_____ 10. All countries must go through a lengthy period
            during which birth rates remain high while
            death rates are low.

Concept Definition: Write the definition of the concept
or term appearing on the left in the blank space next to
it.

1. population density _____

_____

2. migration _____

_____

3. birth rate _____

_____

4. exponential population growth _____

_____

5. open system _____

_____

6. demography _____

_____

7. net immigration _____

_____

8. net migration _____

9. replacement rate _____

_____

10. immigration _____

_____

ANSWERS

Self Quiz

1.	a	6.	d	11.	b	16.	a
2.	b	7.	d	12.	c	17.	b
3.	b	8.	c	13.	c	18.	b
4.	c	9.	c	14.	d	19.	d
5.	c	10.	a	15.	a	20.	a

Concept Recognition

1. biological structure
2. completed fertility rate
3. natural increase rate
4. the demographic transition
5. death rate
6. geometric progression
7. biological evolution
8. gene
9. sensus
10. biological adaptation

True-False

1.	F	6.	T
2.	T	7.	F
3.	F	8.	F
4.	F	9.	T
5.	F	10.	F

Concept Definition

See Glossary in back of this booklet

Human Ecology

18

OVERVIEW

Human ecology, the science of the relationships
between humans and their environment, takes into account
the special abilities we have to resist disorder or entropy by obtaining information feedback from the physical
environment. Sociologists have emphasized spatial relationships within the city. This is illustrated by concentric zone theory, in which there are rings for the
central business district, deteriorating residences,
and so on. Classical and neoclassical ecology focus on
economic and occupational factors. Cultural ecology
centers on norms and values, such as the effective movement to preserve the Boston Common. There is considerable controversy over the existence of limits to economic
growth. Critics of growth focus on problems of pollution
as well as on the depletion of nonrenewable resources.
Others emphasize human capacity to deal with such problems
with the aid of information feedback.

SYNOPSIS

18.1 Physical Structures

Organisms tend to be more negentropic (resist disorder) than nonliving physical structures: they
resist disorder or disorganization to a great

211

extent. Why? They are open systems to a greater
extent, that is, they interact more with their
environment. And that interaction involves information feedbacks, or the flow of knowledge of the
environment to the organism. Cybernetics is a
theory that emphasizes the importance of information feedback for controlling the environment. It
applies to both machines and human beings. Its
applications are illustrated by analyzing what
happens when we drive a car within a traffic lane.
If the car begins to move out of the lane, information to that effect comes to us as a result of
our vision. We then act, on the basis of that information, to control the environment: we turn
the steering wheel in the appropriate direction.
A thermostat operates in a similar fashion. When
a difference between a pre-set temperature and the
environmental temperature is detected (information
feedback), it activates or shuts off an appropriate
heating or cooling unit.

18.2 The Ecology of the City

a Classical Urban Ecology

Sociologists such as Spencer and Sumner attempted
to apply the Darwinian theory of evolution to the
evolution of society. They were interested in the
movement of society toward ever increasing adaptive
capacity. They believed that social change moves
society, inevitably, in a progressive or improved
direction, and that society necessarily passes
through certain stages in a certain direction
(unilinear evolution). Park, Burgess and others
at the University of Chicago were influenced by
these societal evolutionists as they proceeded to
found a school of orban ecology. For example, Park
distinguished between biotic and cultural aspects
of human behavior. The biotic refers to the animal-
istic or competitive struggle, similar to Darwin's
orientation to the survival of the fittest. Three
theories of urban ecology that developed are concentric zone theory (emphasizing rings around the
central business district), sector theory (emphasizing spokes following public transportation
routes), and multiple nuclei theory (centering on
specialized land uses with a variety of points as
their foci).

b   Changes in the Theory of Evolution

Contemporary sociologists have not completely
abandoned the idea of societal evolution. However,
they have modified it so as to focus on multilinear
as distinct from unilinear evolution. No longer
are certain stages or paths seen as inevitable for
all societies, and the idea of inevitability is
gone.

c   Neoclassical Urban Ecology

The early emphasis of Park and others in the Chicago
school of urban ecology on economic factors has not
been abandoned. It is being continued by neoclassical urban ecologists such as Hawley and Duncan
who focus, for example, on the influence of occupational status and place of residence. However,
the earlier distinction between the biotic and
cultural levels has been abandoned.

d   Cultural Ecology

Some contemporary ecologists who focus on noneconomic societal factors use an approach that has
been labeled "cultural ecology." For example,
Firey analyzed the factors which resulted in the
preservation of the Boston Common despite the huge
economic losses involved in routing traffic around
it. He concluded that noneconomic factors--such
as the view of the Common as a sacred object--tri-
umphed over economic ones. Sjoberg's analysis of
the preindustrial city does not separate economic
from noneconomic factors. For example, he emphasizes the importance of technology as well as
highly-developed social structures in the origins
of the preindustrial city.

18.3 Altering Urban Environments

Some residents of Southeast Baltimore have developed
a grass-roots movement to improve their physical
environment. Their approach is entirely different
from slum clearance, as emphasized in many urban
renewal programs. The fight against a proposed
expressway that might have divided the area and
produced considerable pollution was the initial
basis for efforts by the residents to organize
themselves. Subsequently, the Southeast Community
Against the Road (SCAR) grew into the Southeast

213

Community Organization (SECO) which was focused on community restoration. The residents became involved in a variety of activities: working through the city council, securing bank loans, using direct-action confrontations, discouraging the conversion of row houses to flats, obtaining improved city services, homesteading techniques to renovate old houses, and old-fashioned neighborhood boosterism.

18.4 The Growth Controversy

a Are There Limits to Growth?

Attitudes toward the inevitability and importance of continuing industrial growth have begun to shift as a result of problems of obtaining energy and of pollution. There is also growing realization that many of the resources presently being used are non-renewable. Commentators like Schumacher (Small Is Beautiful) have called attention to these problems.

b The M.I.T. Study of Industrial Growth

With the aid of computer simulation techniques (using a computer to derive the implications of certain assumptions), projections for population size, pollution, industrial output, food supply and natural resources have been made by an M.I.T. group. In Limits to Growth they emphasize the importance of curbing continuing economic growth if disasters are to be avoided. Many observers have criticized their conclusions, with a variety of reasons involved. Some believe they are too pessimistic about future scarcities, others point up the vagueness of their concept of "growth," and still others believe that human development--rather than economic growth--should have no limit.

c Analyzing the Growth Controversy

One approach to interpreting the M.I.T. study is to see it as a prediction. Here, it is quite easy to question many things about it. For example, some of its important assumptions can be challenged, and a computer simulation is no better than the assumptions that it carries forward. Another interpretation is to see it as a series of projections based on alternative assumptions. Here, the study can provide us with information as to what might

happen in the future if certain things continued
to remain true (assumptions). With this approach,
this information can be used as the basis of attaining cybernetic control over the environmental
problems involved. Such control is illustrated by
the successes of efforts in the U.S. to control air
pollution based on earlier studies of increases in
air pollution. Another illustration has to do with
present-day efforts to tap solar energy because
of the limited supplies of petroleum, a nonrenewable natural resource.

SELF-QUIZ

Multiple Choice: In the space provided, enter the letter
of the answer that best completes the question.

_____ 1. Urban ecologists focus on

a) the relationships between organisms and
their environment
b) the relationships between human beings and
their environment
c) the relationships people and the environment of the city
d) the relationships among people in the city

_____ 2. Negentropic behavior is aided by

a) information feedback
b) closed systems
c) unbounded systems
d) closed and unbounded systems

_____ 3. Cybernetic principles apply to

a) only human beings
b) only machines
c) both human beings and machines
d) only organisms other than Homo sapiens

_____ 4. Movement toward entropy is best illustrated by

a) a diamond that maintains its characteristics
over the ages
b) a candle that burns down
c) a solar system which continues to follow
the laws of planetary motion
d) a human being who maintains her body temperature

_____ 5. The operation of a thermostat, and the behavior
of an individual driving in a lane, both involve

a) information feedback
b) the operation of cybernetic principles
c) neither of the above
d) both a) and b)

6. Social Darwinism

    a) implies multilinear evolution
    b) implies inevitable progress
    c) implies alternative stages which societies
       might go through
    d) implies that the United States is more
       progressive than the rest of the world

7. The Chicago school of human ecology included

    a) Robert Park
    b) Herbert Spencer
    c) William Graham Sumner
    d) Walter Firey

8. Which theory of urban ecology, developed at
   Chicago, centers on human competition within
   the industrial city:

    a) multiple nuclei theory
    b) sector theory
    c) concentric zone theory
    d) the theory of human ecology

9. The displacement of one ethnic group by another
   best illustrates

    a) closed systems
    b) ecological succession
    c) open systems
    d) bounded systems

10. Biological and societal evolution are related
    in that

    a) both refer to the development of increasing
       dysfunctions
    b) both refer to improved adaptation
    c) neither involves information feedback
    d) both involve cybernetic principles

11. Neoclassical and classical ecology are related
    in that

    a) both emphasize economic factors
    b) both emphasize cultural factors
    c) both distinguish between the biotic and the
       cultural
    d) neither distinguishes between the biotic

and the cultural

_____ 12. Neoclassical and cultural ecology are related in that

a) both emphasize economic factors
b) both emphasize cultural factors
c) both deal equally with economic and cultural factors
d) none of the above

_____ 13. The Boston Common was preserved because, in large measure, of

a) purely economic factors
b) its status as a symbol of historical sentiments
c) it did not interfere with traffic patterns
d) the cost to the taxpayers was inconsequential

_____ 14. Residents of Southeast Baltimore, in attempting to alter their physical environment,

a) set up the Southeast Community Organization
b) helped initiate the construction of a six-lane highway
c) avoided help from the city government
d) avoided help from banks

_____ 15. Southeast Baltimore residents

a) rejected the idea of neighborhood boosterism
b) emphasized ethnic group loyalties and church ties
c) did not utilize information feedback principles
d) did not utilize cybernetic principles

_____ 16. According to the U.S. Bureau of Mines, on the assumption of increasing consumption rates, petroleum will last

a) 345 years
b) 142 years
c) 67 years
d) 20 years

_____ 17. Between 1970 and 1974, with regard to air pollution in the U.S.,

    a) there has been a sharp increase, in general
    b) there has been a slight increase, in general
    c) carbon monoxides have decreased by over 10 percent
    d) there has been no change

_____ 18. The M.I.T. study of industrial growth

    a) used the technique of computer simulation
    b) estimates no real pollution problems involved in continued growth
    c) estimates no real food problem involved in continued growth
    d) estimates no real problem with the using up of natural resources involved in continued growth

_____ 19. Criticism of the M.I.T. study includes the idea that

    a) they limited themselves to closed systems
    b) they limited themselves to unbounded closed systems
    c) they were vague in their definition of "growth"
    d) they failed to make use of cybernetic principles

_____ 20. Nuclear fusion energy, if it is made practical technologically as well as with respect to pollution, can release more energy than this planet's supply of fossil fuels by a factor of

    a) 10
    b) 100
    c) 5,000
    d) 500,000

Concept Recognition: Write the concept or term in the blank space next to its definition.

_____ 1. The study of the noneconomic societal factors involved in the relationships between human beings and their environment.

_____ 2.   A pattern of geographical mobility in which particular ethnic groups or social
classes displace others over time.

_____ 3.   The science of the relationships between organisms and their environment.

_____ 4.   A theory of societal evolution
which holds that social change represents inevitable
progress toward improved human adaptation to the
physical and social environment along a single path.

_____ 5.   Ideas linking human competition
within the industrial city to concentric circles
dividing the city into different areas (corresponding to alternative land uses) on the basis of their
distance from the city's central business district.

_____ 6.   A theory of effective control
of the environment on the basis of information
feedback.

_____ 7.   A process of change which enhances the adaptive capacity of society.

_____ 8.   Those who study the human ecology of life in the city.

_____ 9.   Ideas linking modes of public
transportation to urban patterns best described
by "spokes" radiating from the "hub" of the city
that divide it into areas of differential land use.

_____10.   A procedure utilizing computers
to derive the logical and mathematical implications
of initial assumptions.

True/False: Enter "T" for true or "F" for false for the
best answer to the statement.

_____ 1.   Fully 99.98 percent of the power influx into
the earth's environment comes through solar
radiation.

_____ 2.   Organisms are more negentropic than relatively
closed physical systems.

_____ 3.   The term "cybernetics" was coined by Norbert
Wiener.

_____ 4. Computers are not able to extend the degree to which human beings are open systems.

_____ 5. Social Darwinism has replaced the multilinear theory of evolution.

_____ 6. Robert Park distinguished between the biotic and the cultural.

_____ 7. Concentric zone, sector, and multiple nuclei theories are all theories of urban ecology.

_____ 8. The analysis of both advanced technology and well-developed social structures as factors in the origin of the preindustrial city illustrates neoclassical ecology.

_____ 9. Southeast Baltimore residents found the technique of slum clearance to be highly effective.

_____10. One problem of the M.I.T. study of industrial growth is not taking into account the pressure that rising prices exert on society to look for new alternatives.

Concept Definition: Write the definition of the concept or term appearing on the left in the blank space next to it.

1. second law of thermodynamics _____

_____

2. multilinear evolution _____

_____

3. human ecology _____

_____

4. entropy _____

_____

5. cultural paradigm _____

_____

6. community _____

_____

7. multiple nuclei theory _____

_____

8. cultural paradigm _____

_____

9. physical structures _____

_____

10. unilinear evolution _____

_____

ANSWERS

Self Quiz

1.	c	6.	b	11.	a	16.	d
2.	a	7.	a	12.	d	17.	c
3.	c	8.	c	13.	b	18.	a
4.	b	9.	b	14.	a	19.	c
5.	d	10.	d	15.	b	20.	d

Concept Recognition

1.	cultural ecology	6.	cybernetics
2.	ecological succession	7.	societal evolution
3.	ecology	8.	urban ecologists
4.	Social Darwinism	9.	sector theory
5.	concentric zone theory	10.	computer simulation

True-False

1.	T	6.	T
2.	T	7.	T
3.	T	8.	F
4.	F	9.	F
5.	F	10.	T

Concept Definition

See Glossary in back of this booklet

222

Collective Behavior
19

OVERVIEW

Crowds, mobs, riots, panics, mass hysteria, public opionio, propaganda, social movements--these are phenomena illustrating collective behavior or patterns of behavior with relatively little formal or informal structure. Some of these kinds of behavior are more structured than others, as is the case for social movements (collectivities acting with some continuity to promote or resist change in society). An example is the women's liberation movement, which encompasses both formal organizations like NOW (that give it unity and direction) and informal consciousness-raising groups (that provide it with continuing vitality).

SYNOPSIS

19.1 The Nature of Collective Behavior

  a Definition

Widespread looting during the New York City blackout of 1977 may appear to be "like mad dogs and animals going wild," but there are patterns within this madness. It is such patterns which are the focus of the study of collective behavior: patterns of thinking, feeling and acting. And collective behavior is most obvious in situations (like the blackout) with relatively little formal structure. Thus, for example, more collective behavior can be observed at a rock concert than among soldiers drilling or at a lecture. And the same is true for a crowd at the scene of an accident than a family seated around the dinner table.

b   Collective Behavior and Social Change

The study of collective behavior provides an important opportunity for the analysis of social change. This is in part because of examination of collective behavior alerts us to the sequences of tiny events occurring from one moment to the next.

19.2   Phenomena with Little Structure'

a   Crowds and Mobs

A number of people temporarily gathered together is a crowd. A mob is a crowd organized around a destructive or aggressive goal, as illustrated by the lynch mob attacking a courthouse in Lexington, Kentucky, in 1920. That "acting crowd" may be distinguished from the conventional crowds to be found in classrooms or lecture halls, and also from the expressive crowds in theatres and football stadiums.

b   Riots

A riot is aggressive and destructive behavior generally involving various crowds in different areas. The Watts riot in 1965 was largely triggered by rumors about police brutality, but many other factors were involved. Individuals who passed along such rumors tended to add their own personal definitions of the situation. Some of the individuals who looted explained later that they were making up for the high prices they had been charged for the merchandise as well as for financing practices. Larger societal trends were also involved. For example, the Supreme Court's desegregation decision in 1954 influenced a revolution of rising expectations by blacks. Many of these expectations were subsequently unfulfilled. Yet our knowledge of riots--and collective behavior in general--has serious gaps. We know little about the small-scale interactions, activities, and personal definitions of the situation involved from moment to moment.

c   Panics

Panics occur when people believe they are facing
an immediate and intense threat (whether in fact
such a threat is actually involved). For example,
a "run on a bank" (during a period in history when
deposits were not insured) was precipitated by
fear of losing one's savings. Some people who
gathered at the bank to withdraw their savings
would stimulate others into thinking that the bank
could no longer meet its obligations, and large
crowds would then gather to withdraw their money.
The result was often a self-fulfilling prophesy.
A bank which might initially have been quite sound
became completely unsound as more and more customers
withdrew funds.

d   Mass Hysteria

Mass hysteria is uncoordinated behavior, just as
panic is, but it is widespread, as illustrated by
the results of the Orson Welles radio broadcast
in 1938. Welles' realistic portrayal of the land-
ing of Martian cylinders in New Jersey and the
widespread death and destruction resulting created
mass hysteria among many thousands. These included
educated as well as less-educated individuals.

e   Public Opinion

Mob and panic behavior are associated with strong
expression of emotions, but public opinion is not.
A public is a collectivity or group concerned about
and divided over a given issue; thus, for every
issue there is a particular public. And the
attitudes of a public is public opinion. A study
of the 1940 U.S. presidential election uncovered a
"two-step flow" in opinion formation: (1) from the
mass media to "opinion leaders," and (2) from opinion leaders to others. Another study showed the
centrality of face-to-face contacts in the formation of opinion. Other factors are involved as
well, such as widespread movements like the women's
movement.

f   Propaganda

Propaganda is one-sided information focused on the

persuasion of a public concerning some issue or opinion. It may be true or false, but it is always one-sided, as distinct from balanced. It contrasts with our ideals for scientific communication. Propaganda techniques are illustrated in Sociological Consciousness 6-1 and 6-2 (Section 6.1). For example, there are the techniques of repetition and proof by selected instances.

19.3 Social Movements

a   Formal and Informal Structure within Social Movements

Social movements are more structured than other forms of collective behavior. They act with some degree of continuity to promote or resist change in society. Some are more revolutionary, or oriented to fundamental social change, than others. The origin of women's liberation is based on many factors, but one event involved occurred in 1967 in Chicago at the National Conference for New Politics. A sexist remark along with sexist behavior by the chairman helped to precipitate the formation of the first locally-organized independent group of women in the movement. It is a movement that includes relatively formal organizations like NOW along with grassroots consciousness-raising or political groups like the one referred to above.

b   The Career of Social Movements

A series of stages which many social movements undergo may be distinguished. With respect to the New Left movement, there are these stages: (1) incipiency, occurring in the mid- or late-1950s during the earliest days in the civil rights movement; (2) coalescence, in the early 1960s with the rise of Students for a Democratic Society (SDS) and the Student Nonviolent Coordinating Committee (SNCC), and with the New Frontier and War on Poverty mentality of the Kennedy administration; (3) institutionalization, beginning in early 1965, with the massive focus on ending the war in Vietnam; (4) fragmentation (now occurring--as of 1971-- according to Mauss); and (5) demise.

c   Goal and Means Displacement

The decline of SDS illustrates the process of goal

displacement: a desire for continuing growth and respectability displaced the original radical ideals. The process illustrates Michels' "iron law of oligarchy." Means displacement is illustrated by the Women's Christian Temperance Unions choice to remain outside the mainstream of Protestant thought rather than give up on its goals. Organizational means did not displace the ideals of the movement.

d   Social Movements and Mass Society

Mass society refers to people relatively isolated from one another rather than relating within broad groupings such as social classes or political parties. According to some sociologists, it is the isolated individual--the person who feels most alienated--who is most likely to join mass social movements. Other sociologists emphasize the importance of a pre-existing communications network for a social movement to develop, as in the origins of women's liberation. These two ideas are not necessarily contradictory, since alienation from established organizations can occur at the same time as informal communication networks centered on changing the establishment are developing. And both can contribute to the origins of a social movement.

SELF-QUIZ

Multiple Choice: In the space provided, enter the letter
of the answer that best completes the question.

_____ 1. Collectivities and aggregates are related in
that

     a) both necessarily consist of people congre-
gated or found together
     b) both are types of social categories
     c) both are types of groups
     d) none of the above

_____ 2. Which best illustrates a situation where collective behavior occurs:

     a) a factory
     b) soldiers drilling
     c) a playground
     d) a lecture hall

_____ 3. Informal and formal structures are related in
that

     a) the less of both, the greater the chances
for collective behavior
     b) the more of both, the greater the changes
for collective behavior
     c) there is no formal and informal structure
in situations where collective behavior
takes place
     d) none of the above

_____ 4. Which of these concepts emphasizes a low degree of social structure:

     a) role
     b) social stratification system
     c) social relationship
     d) social change

_____ 5. Which of these concepts emphasizes a high degree of social structure:

     a) classless society
     b) primary group
     c) unanticipated consequences of purposive
action
     d) role conflict

6. The Kentucky riot of 1920 included

   a) an attempt by a mob to lynch a black man
   b) a newsreel photographer leading the charge
   c) the refusal of white soldiers to fire on
      the crowd
   d) the lynching of a black man

7. A crowd at Yankee Stadium is

   a) an expressive crowd
   b) a casual crowd
   c) an acting crowd
   d) a conventional crowd

8. Rumors

   a) are necessarily false
   b) do not distort information in a random or
      haphazard fashion
   c) are of known origin
   d) are transmitted by formal structures

9. During the Watts riot of 1965,

   a) looting was infrequent
   b) definite relationships to societal trends
      were uncovered
   c) a key rumor was that a white woman assaulted
      a black man
   d) a key rumor was that a pregnant woman was
      beaten by black police

10. According to McPhail, who reviewed ten studies
    of riots,

    a) a sociological theory of how riots start
       can now be constructed
    b) riots are the product of downtrodden people
    c) riots are closely associated with mob-dis-
       persal techniques
    d) little is known about the small-scale inter-
       actions and personal definitions of the
       situation occurring in riots

11. A panic and mass hysteria both

    a) are characterized by uncoordinated behavior
    b) are behavior within organizations
    c) are widespread behavior

d) occur in one particular place

_____ 12. Orson Welles' dramatization of an invasion
from Mars

    a) resulted in panic but not mass hysteria
    b) was frightening primarily to working-class
       people
    c) provoked mass hysteria
    d) was frightening primarily to middle-class
       people

_____ 13. Mob behavior, panic behavior and public opinion
are related in that

    a) they all tend to occur in formally struc-
       tured situations
    b) they all tend to occur in informally struc-
       tured situations
    c) mob and panic behavior are associated with
       strong emotions to a greater extent than
       public opinion
    d) all are irrational modes of behavior

_____ 14. According to a study of opinion leaders by
Katz and Lazarsfeld,

    a) there are two types: influentials and
       associates
    b) they are all face-to-face contacts
    c) there are two types: leaders and co-leaders
    d) there are two types: step one, and step
       two

_____ 15. Propaganda and rumor are related in that

    a) both are false
    b) both are almost completely true
    c) both are designed to persuade people to
       adopt a certain opinion
    d) both may be true, false or some mixture

_____ 16. "The Talk of the 70s" is propagandistic because

    a) it has many cliches
    b) it is very one-sided
    c) the values behind it are unproven
    d) it is not based on a probability sample

_____ 17. A revolution and a social movement are related
in that

a) a social movement is a type of revolution
b) both are completely unstructured
c) both are completely structured
d) a revolution is a type of social movement

_____ 18. In comparing social movements and mob behavior,

a) social movements tend to have more formal structure
b) both have no informal structure
c) neither has any formal structure
d) both are highly irrational

_____ 19. The formation of Chicago's first locally organized independent women's liberation group

a) took place in 1952
b) grew out of the New Left movement after women were treated in sexist ways
c) grew out of the American communist movement
d) occurred as a result of the interests of housewives who were not politically oriented

_____ 20. Means displacement is best illustrated by

a) the New Left movement
b) the women's liberation movement
c) the Women's Christian Temperance Union
d) the black movement

Concept Recognition: Write the concept or term in the blank space next to its definition.

_____ 1. A crowd organized around a specific aggressive or destructive goal.

_____ 2. A dispersed grouping or collectivity concerned with and divided over an issue.

_____ 3. Every large organization, no matter how egalitarian its principles, must establish a bureaucracy with a few leaders monopolizing power.

_____ 4. Information of unknown origin that is communicated through informal structure.

_____ 5. The patterns of thinking, feeling and acting of people in groups with relatively little formal or informal social structure.

_____ 6. Widespread uncoordinated behavior of collectivities or individuals who believe
they face an immediate and intense threat.

_____ 7. Aggressive and destructive crowd
behavior.

_____ 8. Any set of individuals considered together as a single unit.

_____ 9. Uncoordinated behavior of a
group who believe they face an immediate and intense threat.

_____10. A collectivity acting with some
continuity to promote or resist a change in the
society or group of which it is a part.

True/False: Enter "T" for true or "F" for false for the
best answer to the statement.

_____ 1. The New Left movement, according to Mauss, was
            in a stage of fragmentation in 1971.

_____ 2. Social movements, in comparison to other kinds
            of collective behavior, emphasize both formal
            and informal structure.

_____ 3. Revolutions are necessarily violent.

_____ 4. Scientific communication is a kind of propaganda.

_____ 5. The "two-step flow" in the effect of media on
            political opinions refers to the two stages
            through which individuals pass as their opin-
            ions are altered.

_____ 6. In the Orson Welles' dramatization of an inva-
            sion from Mars, the Martians had landed in
            Detroit.

_____ 7. A run on a bank is used by Merton to illus-
            trate the self-fulfilling prophesy.

_____ 8. An example of a casual crowd is students in
            a seminar.

_____ 9. An example of a conventional crowd is the
            audience at a public lecture.

_____10. A newsreel cameraman helped to start the charge
on the Kentucky Courthouse in the 1920 riot
there.

Concept Definition: Write the definition of the concept
or term appearing on the left in the blank space next to
it.

1. revolution _____

_____

2. alienation _____

_____

3. propaganda _____

_____

4. means displacement _____

_____

5. crowd _____

_____

6. public opinion _____

_____

7. self-fulfilling prophesy _____

_____

8. goal displacement _____

_____

9. mass society _____

_____

10. issues _____

_____

ANSWERS

Self Quiz

1.	d	6.	a	11.	a	16.	b
2.	c	7.	a	12.	c	17.	d
3.	a	8.	b	13.	c	18.	a
4.	d	9.	b	14.	b	19.	b
5.	b	10.	d	15.	d	20.	c

Concept Recognition

1. mob
2. public
3. iron law of oligarchy
4. rumor
5. collective behavior

6. mass hysteria
7. riot
8. collectivity
9. panic
10. social movement

True-False

1.	T	6.	F
2.	T	7.	T
3.	F	8.	F
4.	F	9.	T
5.	F	10.	T

Concept Definition

See Glossary in back of this booklet

Theories of
Social Change
20

OVERVIEW

　　Evolutionary theory and cyclical theory are sweeping theories of social change, with the former focusing
on change in a positive direction and the latter illustrated by Toynbee's and Spengler's views of the rise and
fall of societies.　Structural-functional and conflict
theories are less sweeping and provide conceptual tools
for dealing with specific situations.　Micro-theories
(symbolic interactionism, exchange theory and ethnomethodology) deal with change in personalities and small
groups.　Women's liberation illustrates the importance
of both small groups and large organizations in effect-
ing societal change.　Their effectiveness, as well as
the process of societal change in general, is partly
based on images of the future.

SYNOPSIS

20.1 Is Knowledge of Social Change Harmful?

　a　Dangers of Social Science Knowledge

　　　Although all of sociology bears on social change
　　　at least indirectly, and although social change
　　　has been a topic throughout the preceding chapters,
　　　it is useful to develop a more systematic focus.

But prior to such discussions, we might inquire as
to whether it is dangerous to study social change.
George Orwell in his science fiction classic, <u>1984</u>,
described a totalitarianism so extreme that no
individual could resist complete obedience and even
love for the dictator, Big Brother. Will social
science knowledge be used to help establish such
a state?

b   Unanticipated Consequences of Problem-Solving
    Efforts

Social science knowledge may prove to be harmful
even with the best of intentions. This idea is
supported by the concept of the "unanticipated
consequences of purposive action." For example,
Michel's iron law of oligarchy points up the decline of ideals within reformist organizations as
a result of their commitment to strengthen themselves.

c   Constructive Aspects of Social Change

Granting that social science knowledge may be harmful, the alternative is ignorance, and ignorance
may be quite harmful. If we can genuinely learn
about human behavior and social change, then that
learning may help us more than actions on the basis
of ignorance. By avoiding the risks associated
with the development of knowledge, we also avoid
the "risk" of finding paths for dealing with the
major world and personal problems that exist. Scientific knowledge is a "two-edged sword."

20.2 Change in Society as a Whole

a   Evolutionary Theory

In Sections 17.1 and 18.2 biological evolution and
Social Darwinism were discussed, respectively. The
ideas of Charles Darwin have had a great impact on
the world, and it is little wonder that they have
been influential among some sociologists. The
early approach to evolution within sociology, illustrated by the work of Spencer and Sumner, emphasized
the inevitability of progress and the necessity
that all societies move through the same stages.
Currently, sociologists interested in evolutionary
theory are oriented to a multilinear (as distinct
from a unilinear) approach: there are many paths
a society can take to improve its adaptation. A

236

major problem with evolutionary theory is the difficulty of applying it to concrete situations because of its vague concepts.

b Cyclical Theory

Cyclical theory challenges the Social Darwinist idea that progress is inevitable. Spengler, for example, writes of the inevitable birth and decay of civilizations in his Decline of the West. And Toynbee's A Study of History refers to the survival of civilizations as based on their "responses" to the "challenges" presented to them by events. This "challenge and response" approach is analogous to the scientific method.

c Structural-Functional Theory

Structural-functional theory was discussed in some detail in Section 5.2. Its focus is on the contributions to society resulting from group or individual behavior. If changes such as women's liberation or the New Left movement are to achieve success, the structural-functionalist would argue that they must contribute a good deal. And it is even worse for those movements which create "dysfunctions," that is, results harmful to society in some ways. Structural-functionalism is less grandiose than evolutionary or cyclical theory and, thus, can be more easily applied to concrete phenomena.

d Conflict Theory

Conflict theory, discussed in Section 5.3, focuses on the mutual opposition of large scale social structures, as illustrated by Marx's emphasis on the class struggle in history. Other conflict theorists, such as Dahrendorf, are also interested in other kinds of large-scale conflicts, such as religious, racial, political and international conflict. And still other conflict theorists focus on small groups. For example, Simmel's analysis indicates that conflict withiin such groups is essential for the group's continued health.

20.3 Micro-Theory: Symbolic Interactionism, Exchange Theory and Ethnomethodology

A great many of the concepts developed by sociolo-

gists focus on the individual or the small group
setting rather than society as a whole. These are
illustrated by such concepts as self-image, definition of the situation, role distance, relative
deprivation and charismatic authority. The theoretical orientations most concerned with this micro
level of analysis are symbolic interactionism, exchange theory and ethnomethodology. They can help
yield insight, for example, into the successes of
the women's liberation movement. Small consciousness-raising groups appear to have been vitally
important in the achievement of those successes
along with factors operating on a large-scale level
(such as the NOW organization).

20.4 Some Contemporary Images of the Future

What are our images of the future? Images of the
future have a great impact on the shaping of the
future, working like definitions of the situation
to help create the situation. Three illustrations
of images are given: images implied by questions
about the future which high-school students asked,
the image conveyed in a short fictional piece on
the Jetsons (the TV series) written by my ten-year-
old son, and the images conveyed in a Boston Globe
edition dated 2076 to commemorate the bicentennial
year. All of these images, despite the gadgetry
involved in many, are quite traditional. They focus
on material changes rather than fundamental changes
in social or personality structures. They merely
extrapolate existing societal trends.

20.5 Constructing Alternative Images of the Future

Fred Polak's analysis of images of the future in
Western society was presented in Section 11.3. He
concludes that we have lost faith in the traditional
Judeo-Christian image but failed to create any
alternative. By so doing, he believes, we are
failing to develop the necessary solutions to the
problems we face. Yet the creation of new images
of the future that are widely shared appears to
be an immensely difficult task. This is illustrated
by Flatland, the science fiction story presented
in Section 1.1. There, the square who learned of
a three-dimensional world was thrown into prison
for his heresy.

Sociology has not created any unified image of the
future that will solve our problems. But it does

238

provide us with ideas that can be used as tools for constructing such a future. And it does give us methods for testing our ideas against our experiences. Yet what sociology presently offers to us may prove to be only a minute portion of what it will offer in the future.

Multiple Choice: In the space provided, enter the letter of the answer that best completes the question.

_____ 1. Orwell's <u>1984</u> best illustrates the idea that

    a) goal displacement is a common occurrence
    b) knowledge can be used to dehumanize the individual
    c) the revolution of rising expectations is a powerful force
    d) means displacement is a common occurrence

_____ 2. Systematic knowledge from the social sciences can be applied

    a) without unanticipated consequences
    b) with little risk of unanticipated consequences
    c) with substantial risk of unanticipated consequences
    d) with full knowledge of consequences

_____ 3. Evolutionary theory was partly developed by

    a) Simmel
    b) Marx
    c) Toynbee
    d) Spencer

_____ 4. Social Darwinism emphasizes

    a) unilinear evolution
    b) multilinear evolution
    c) biological evolution
    d) biological adaptation

_____ 5. Evolutionary theory

    a) is illustrated by Spengler's <u>Decline of the West</u>
    b) is illustrated by Toynbee's <u>A Study of History</u>
    c) cannot easily be applied to particular situations
    d) implies the development of a classless society

_____ 6. The "challenge and response" idea is characteristic of

a) conflict theory
b) cyclical theory
c) structural-functionalism
d) evolutionary theory

_____ 7. Which of these theoretical orientations is
not generally at a very high level of abstrac-
tion:

a) evolutionary theory
b) cyclical theory
c) Social Darwinism
d) exchange theory

_____ 8. In the analogy between the scientific method
and the challenge-and-response orientation:

a) defining a problem is associated with
challenge
b) testing hypotheses is associated with
challenge
c) analyzing results is associated with challenge
d) constructing hypotheses is associated with
response

_____ 9. A focus on the contributions of the New Left
to society best illustrates which approach:

a) conflict theory
b) evolutionary theory
c) structural-functionalism
d) evolutionary theory

_____ 10. A conclusion that the failure of the counterculture movement to grow because of i-s opposition to fundamental societal institutions best
illustrates which theoretical orientation:

a) structural-functionalism
b) evolutionary theory
c) micro-theory
d) conflict theory

_____ 11. Marxist theory directs our attention primarily
to

a) conflicts within the small group
b) class conflicts
c) religious and racial conflicts
d) conflicts between political parties and
   among nations

_____ 12. The functions of social conflict in the small
group are emphasized by

a) Spencer and Sumner
b) Spengler and Toynbee
c) Simmel and Coser
d) none of the above

_____ 13. Which of these concepts emphasizes personality
structure most:

a) birth rate
b) dysfunctions
c) conforming behavior
d) definition of the situation

_____ 14. Which of these concepts emphasizes social
structure most:

a) cultural paradigm
b) role accumulation
c) charismatic authority
d) role distance

_____ 15. Micro-theory includes

a) Social Darwinism
b) structural-functionalism
c) symbolic interactionism
d) cyclical theory

_____ 16. Which theoretical orientation emphasizes
language most:

a) ethnomethodology
b) conflict theory
c) cyclical theory
d) evolutionary theory

_____ 17. A widespread image of the future

a) completely shapes the future
b) cannot be a self-fulfilling prophesy
c) exerts important influence on the future

d) has very little impact on the future

_____ 18. The questions about the future conveyed by
high school students, used as an illustration
in the text,

a) were extremely abstract
b) emphasized material problems
c) implied an interest in radical social
change
d) implied an interest in radical personality
change

_____ 19. The "news stories" in the <u>Boston Globe</u> about
life in 2076

a) did not deal with new gadgets
b) did not deal with new medical techniques
c) extended existing social trends
d) suggested fundamental changes in social
structure

_____ 20. Fred Polak's view of the Judeo-Christian image
of the future is that

a) it needs to be applied if we are to solve
problems
b) it provides a firm basis for life in the
future
c) it has always meant trouble for Western
society
d) we have lost faith in it, and this limits
the possibilities of our future development

Concept Recognition: Write the concept or term in the
blank space next to its definition.

_____ 1. A theoretical orientation emphasizing the opposition among individuals, groups
or social structures.

_____ 2. A theoretical orientation emphasizing the improving adaptation of society to
its environment as a mechanism of societal change.

_____ 3. A vision of a possible future
reality for society and the individual.

_____ 4. An explanation of history on the

basis of the rise and fall of societies.

_____ 5.   A theoretical orientation emphasizing the functions or contributions made to society by existing social structures.

True/False: Enter "T" for true or "F" for false for the best answer to the statement.

_____ 1.   The sharp increase in the percentage of those 5-19 years old who attend school illustrates social change, directly or indirectly.

_____ 2.   The sharp increase in the percentage of households with television sets illustrates social change, directly or indirectly.

_____ 3.   Sumner was a cyclical theorist.

_____ 4.   Orwell's 1984 has a happy ending.

_____ 5.   There is little danger from the application of social science knowledge.

_____ 6.   Evolutionary theory centers on particular parts of society rather than on society as a whole.

_____ 7.   Cyclical theory questions the inevitability of progress.

_____ 8.   Conflict theory can alert us to fundamental cleavages among values.

_____ 9,   The concept "charismatic authority" emphasizes personality structure more than the concept "traditional authority."

Concept Definition: Write the definition of the concept or term appearing on the left in the blank space next to it.

1.   cyclical theory of history _____

_____

2.   conflict theory _____

_____

3. image of the future _____

_____

4. structural-functionalism _____

_____

5. evolutionary theory _____

_____

ANSWERS

Self Quiz

1.	b	6.	b	11.	b	16.	a
2.	c	7.	d	12.	c	17.	c
3.	d	8.	a	13.	d	18.	b
4.	a	9.	c	14.	a	19.	c
5.	c	10.	a	15.	c	20.	d

Concept Recognition

1. conflict theory
2. evolutionary theory
3. image of the future
4. cyclical theory of history
5. structural-functionalism

True-False

1.	T	6.	F
2.	T	7.	T
3.	F	8.	T
4.	F	9.	T
5.	F		

Concept Definition

See Glossary in back of this booklet

Glossary

abnormal division of labor low degree of communication among specialists

account a commonsense or folk explanation for past occurrences

activity theory a theory stressing the importance for the individual of continuing patterns of activity or involvement into later life

age role a social role associated with a given chronological age

age-role continuity persistent or gradual changes in age roles with advancing chronological age

age-role discontinuity sharply altered age roles with advancing chronological age

age-role pluralism a pattern of age role relations where each age role retains its fundamental values and norms yet incorporates elements from the others

ageism prejudice or discrimination against members of a given age category

agencies of socialization social structures taking part in the socialization process

aggregate a set of individuals congregated together

alienation feelings of powerlessness, meaninglessness, and social isolation associated with certain social relationships

amalgamation the mixing of cultures (and sometimes races as well) so as to form a new culture (and sometimes a new racial type)

anticipatory socialization the learning of future roles or patterns of behavior

arithmetic progression a series of terms in which each term is the sum of the immediately preceding terms and a constant

assimilation the process by which an ethnic culture is altered in important respects so as to conform to a dominant culture

authority legitimate power

bias one-sidedness or prejudice

biological adaptation genetic changes which improve the ability of organisms to adjust to the environment or alter it to adjust to themselves

biological evolution a process of change in the biological structure from generation to generation

biological structure a bounded and relatively open system with the capacity to reproduce itself

birth rate $\dfrac{\text{registered births}}{\text{midyear population}} \times 1{,}000$

bounded system a system located in time and space

bourgeoisie owners of the productive resources

bracketing the suspension of belief in existing assumptions

bureaucracy an organization with an extensive hierarchy and division of labor governed by explicit rules

caste a social category with membership ascribed or determined at birth

caste system a social stratification system in which no (or almost no) mobility from one social category (caste) to another is possible

census a complete count of a population

charismatic authority rule based on belief in the extraordinary personal qualities of the ruler

chronological age age in years

church an organization designed to deal with

the religious needs of the masses in society

class (or social class) (1) (Based on Weber) a social category with its members in the same economic situation (2) (Based on Marx) a social category whose members have a similar relationship to the means of production and who, at some point, develop class consciousness

class consciousness awareness of membership in a class with its associated inequalities and political role

class system a social stratification system in which a greater or lesser degree of mobility from one social category (class) to another is possible

classless society a society with no structured social inequality

closed system a system which does not interact with its environment

coercive organization an organization in which membership is obtained or maintained by force

collective behavior the patterns of thinking, feeling, and acting of people in groups with relatively little formal or informal social structure

collectivity any set of individuals considered together as a single unit

communal family several nuclear families usually not related by blood living together and sharing everything except sexual relations

community a group occupying a territory who share sufficiently wide-ranging goals so that the individual's life may be lived wholly within that area

community-like group any group that emerges without having been deliberately constructed to seek specific goals

community social profile a community reconnaissance undertaken by a small group of researchers who interview key people and analyze available documents to outline the general patterns of community social relationships, values, and norms

competitive relationships relationships in which people are rivals for scarce resources

completed fertility rate (cfr) the average number of births per woman throughout her lifetime

computer simulation a procedure utilizing computers to derive the logical and mathematical implications of initial assumptions

concentric zone theory ideas linking human competition within the industrial city to concentric circles dividing the city into different areas (corresponding to alternative land uses) on the basis of their distance from the city's central business district

conflict theory a theoretical orientation emphasizing the opposition among individuals, groups, or social structures

conforming behavior behavior falling inside the acceptable range according to societal or group norms and values

conspicuous consumption obvious waste or use of valued goods as a means of gaining reputability

conspicuous leisure avoidance of productive work to symbolize the achievement of social status

constructing reality everyday actions which shape phenomena

continuing socialization socialization beyond the early years, which further shapes personality and transmits culture

contest mobility a pattern of educational mobility in which the individual attempts to achieve elite status by means of open contests which mcontinue over a period of time

contract marriage a marriage in which mutual rights and obligations are defined by means of a formal, written marriage contract

control procedures techniques designed to prevent outside factors from interfering with the hypotheses being tested

counterculture a subculture focused on opposition to the culture prevailing in society as a whole

counterintuitive behavior behavior different from commonsense expectations

credentialism a pattern of accepting formal symbols of educational achievement as proof of actual educational achievement

crime that portion of deviant behavior which is in violation of existing laws

crowd a number of people gathered together temporarily

cultural change alteration of culture in a given direction

cultural contact interaction among people of different cultures

cultural ecology the study of the noneconomic societal factors involved in the relationships between human beings and their environment

cultural paradigm a set of explicit and implicit assumptions on which a culture is based

cultural pluralism a pattern of ethnic group relations in which each ethnic group retains its fundamental values and norms yet incorporates certain elements from the others

cultural relativism a tendency to view people's behavior from the perspective of their own culture

culture (1) a blueprint or design for living in society (2) a system of expectations and goals widely shared within society (3) a system of norms and values

culture of poverty a culture arising from economic poverty and characterized by isolation, dependence, and hopelessness

culture of silence a culture characterized by a lack of self-expression in thought or speech

cybernetics a theory of effective control of the environment on the basis of information feedback

cyclical theory of history an explanation of history on the basis of the rise and fall of societies

death rate registered deaths $\times 1,000$ midyear population

definition of a research problem a statement that specifies (1) a focus on certain phenomena, (2) particular concepts or theories to be used, and (3) general procedures for collecting evidence

definition of the situation the shaping of behavior through interpreting the past and outlining directions for the future

degradation ceremony a pattern of action stripping the individual of aspects of self-image or identity

demographic transition the change from high to low birth and death rates accompanying industrialization

demography the science of human population

dependent variable a variable which changes in response to changes in an independent variable

deviance amplification a mutual-causal relationship producing increasing deviance

deviance counteraction a mutual-causal relationship producing decreasing deviance

deviant behavior behavior falling outside the acceptable range according to societal or group nnorms and values

direct relationship between two variables the variables change in the same direction

discrimination actions creating disadvantages for members of an ethnic group compared with others

disengagement theory a theory emphasizing an inevitable mutual withdrawal, arising gradually, between the aging person and others

division of labor specialization among tasks organized around a central goal

dysfunctions a social structure's consequences for society which lessen society's adaptation or adjustment

dystopia a negative image of the future

ecological succession a pattern of geographical mobility in which particular ethnic groups of social classes displace others over time

ecology the science of the relationships between organisms and their environment

economic institution the social structure centering on the production, distribution, and use of wealth

educational institution the social structure that emphasizes the communication of knowledge

educational meritocracy an educational system with equal opportunity for all students to rise on the basis of academic performance

emigration the movement of people out of a country

entropy the extent of disorder in a system

equalitarian society the structuring of social equality in society as a whole

equality of opportunity a situation in which all members of society have equal or similar opportunities to attain positions on the higher levels of the stratification system

ethnic group a set of individuals who see themselves or are seen by others as belonging to a certain social category because of their common ancestry

ethnic stratification system a hierarchy of ethnic groups which structures social inequality

ethnicity degree of identification by self or others with an ethnic group

ethnocentrism a tendency to understand the world only from the viewpoint of one's own culture

ethnomethodology a theoretical orientation aimed at describing how people in everyday interactions construct definitions of the situation and shape reality

ethnotheories commonsense or folk theories about how to solve problems

evidence information or data that can be used to evaluate or test hypotheses or theories

evolutionary theory a theoretical orientation emphasizing the improving adaptation of society to its environment as a mechanism of societal change

exchange theory a theoretical orientation emphasizing the goals, rewards, and punishments associated with interaction

expectation belief or prediction

expectations beliefs implying "should" or "should not"

experiment a procedure for collecting information through (1) actively changing a situation, such as altering the independent variable, and (2) systematically recording results obtained under two or more conditions, such as assessing changes in the dependent variable

exploitation of others making use of others for unethical or selfish purposes

exponential population growth population growth obased on a geometric progression

expressive orientation an emphasis on immediate gratification of desires rather than making progress toward future goals

extended family two or more nuclear families and three or more generations, generally living together

faith deep emotional conviction

family a social structure made up of people related by blood, marriage, or adoption

folkways norms generally regarded as useful but not essential for society

force physical coercion or the threat of such coercion

formal rationality the association of accurate calculations with alternative actions

formal structure the explicit goals and rules for behavior

functions a social structure's consequences for society which improve society's adaptation or adjustment

garden city a community surrounded by a belt of agriculture with a maximum population of 30,000 people

gemeinschaft a social structure emphasizing close personal relationships

gender the inherited or biological characteristics distinguishing one sex from the other

gene a fundamental hereditary unit in all organisms that influences biological structure and is capable of mutation or change

generalized other the organization of the attitudes of the group as a whole

generation unit an age group with a common social and historical experience and similar norms, values, and patterns of behavior

geometric progression a series of terms in which each term is a constant multiple of the immediately preceding term

gesellschaft a social structure emphasizing transitory and impersonal relationships

goal displacement the replacement of one goal or value by another

goals interests or preferences existing at different levels of the individual's awareness

gross national product (GNP) the dollar value attached to all the goods and services produced in a society

group a set of individuals who define themselves as a group or are so defined by others

group marriage a marriage in which several nuclear families usually not related by blood live together and share everything including sexual relations

Hawthorne effect an improvement in performance based on the effect of scientific research

Homo sapiens the human organism

homosexual marriage the union of two individuals of the same sex

horizontal pattern of a community the interrelationship among social structures on approximately the same hierarchical level within the community

human ecology the science of the relationships between human beings and their environment

humanistic oriented toward helping people achieve their highest potentialities

hypothesis a tentative idea or statement about how to solve a problem or about the nature of reality

I an aspect of the personality expressing the individual's uniqueness

ideal type a description of a pure type or extreme case in order to highlight key features

image of the future a vision of a possible future reality for society and the individual

immigration the movement of people into a country

independent variable a variable which, as it changes, influences changes in a dependent variable

industrial society a society in which a substantial proportion of the labor force is involved in the production of goods

influence the ability to control the behavior of others beyond any authority to do so

informal structure the actual pattern of behavior and the values and norms associated with that behavior

information feedback data flowing from the environment to the organism

instincts patterns of behavior that are biologically fixed and universal for a species

institution a social structure built around certain values and tending to persist over time

institutionalization coordination within any one relatively stable social structure focused on certain values

instrumental orientation a focus on attaining some future goal and on action as a means of attaining it

intelligence capacity for learning

intergenerational mobility mobility from one generation to the next

interview schedules guides for interviewing, which include questions to be asked

interview survey a procedure for collecting information by interviewing people (asking questions and recording answers)

intragenerational mobility mobility within the lifetime of the individual

inverse relationship between two variables the variables change in opposite directions

investigator effect the influence of a scientist on his or her research

iron law of oligarchy the principle that every large organization, no matter how egalitarian its ideals, must establish a bureaucracy with a few leaders monopolizing power

issues problems that involve the interest of collectivities or individuals in society

label assign to a social category

language a system of symbols that helps people to communicate past experiences and apply them to the present

latent functions functions which are neither intended nor recognized

laws norms formally chosen to be backed up by punishments for failure to conform to them, with particular social agencies designated to do the enforcing

learning a relatively permanent change in behavior that occurs as a result of experience

legal authority rule based on law or formal decrees and regulations

legitimation the justification of behavior on the basis of cultural or subcultural values and norms

linguistic relativity hypothesis the idea that a given language tends to cause people to understand the world in a certain way

looking-glass self the reactions of others to our own behavior, which function as a kind of mirror reflecting back to us and contributes to the process by which the self is formed

major theoretical orientations perspectives that link together a large number of concepts, hypotheses, and theories

manifest functions functions which are intended and recognized

mass hysteria widespread uncoordinated behavior of collectivities or individuals who believe they face an immediate and intense threat

mass society a society made up of people who are not integrated into broad groupings such as social classes or political parties

me an aspect of the personality expressing the attitudes of others

means displacement rigid adherence to a goal with little regard to finding adequate means for attaining it

mechanical solidarity feelings of togetherness based on the similarity of work

megalopolis a region consisting of several large cities and their surrounding areas that make up a single urban complex

metropolitan areas urban areas which include one or more central cities, suburban areas, and satellite cities

migration the physical movement of population from one area to another

mob a crowd organized around a specific aggressive or destructive goal

mores norms generally regarded as essential for the welfare of society

multilinear evolution societal evolution along multiple paths

multiple nuclei theory ideas emphasizing a tendency for similar land uses to cluster around a series of nuclei, each with its own specialized activities

mutual-causal relationship a relationship between two factors in which each continues to affect the other

natural increase rate birthrate minus death rate

net immigration immigration less emigration

net migration migration into an area minus migration out of it

norm an expectation widely shared within society (or a subgroup of society)

normal division of labor high degree of communication among specialists

normative conflict the conflict inherent in norms involving contradictory expectations

nuclear family a family made up of parents and their children

objectivity an unprejudiced orientation or openness to information about the true nature of reality

observation a procedure for collecting information by informally recording descriptions of behavior seen or observed, or by systematically recording descriptions designed to test particular hypotheses

open system a system in interaction with its environment

operational definitions procedures for measuring the phenomena to which a concept refers

organic solidarity feelings of togetherness based on a division of labor

organization a group deliberately constructed to seek specific goals.

panic uncoordinated behavior of a collectivity or grouping who believe they face an immediate and intense threat

paradigm a system of explicit and implicit assumptions on which a science is based

paternalistic relationships relationships in which one group is subservient to another, given little responsibility, and has its basic needs provided for

peer groups a group of similar age and background (to those of the individual in question)

permeable usage a usage of a concept so that there is openness to new information

personality structure (1) the individual's system rof roles organized around a self-image (2) the individual's system of expectations, goals, and actions that has persisted over time

physical structures bounded systems of matter

plausibility structure the patterns of social relationships which support a given world view or definition of social reality

pluralist approach to power an orientation which emphasizes the existence of competition among elites which check and balance one another so that no one elite attains dominance

political institution the social structure centering on the development, distribution, and use of power

political orientation the stress on such phenomena as law, power, authority, and influence

population density population size per unit of land area

postindustrial society a society in which the percentage of those employed in agriculture stabilizes at a very low level, with a continuing decrease of the percentage in manufacturing and increase of the percentage in services

power the ability to control the behavior of others—against their will if necessary—by using force, authority, or influence

power-elite approach an orientation which sees power as held by an elite who are at the top of multiple dimensions of stratification

power-structure approach an orientation which views power as stemming primarily or exclusively from stratification in terms of wealth

pragmatism a philosophy which focuses on the practical outcomes which ideas, in general, and science and technology, in particular, have on human affairs

precision of measurement the smallest interval a measurement is able to detect—that is, accuracy of measurement

preindustrial society a society in which the vast majority of the population is engaged in agriculture

prejudice negative beliefs or expectations and feelings directed against members of an ethnic group

preliterate having no written language

primary group a face-to-face group that is fundamental in forming the personality structure of its members

primary socialization the initial socialization which is primarily responsible for the formation of personality and the transmission of culture

probability sampling a sampling procedure

in which each individual or unit has a known probability of being chosen

progressive education a system of education stressing the cultivation of individuality, spontaneous student activities, learning through experience, and the importance of understanding the changing world

proletariat workers employed by the owners

propaganda one-sided information designed to persuade a public to adopt a particular opinion

Protestant ethic a system of values linked to Calvinist theology emphasizing hard work, thrift, and the accumulation of wealth

public a dispersed grouping or collectivity concerned with and divided over an issue

public opinion the attitudes of a public

Pygmalion effect the development of a more favorable self-image, along with behavior appropriate to that image, based on changes in the expectations of significant others

questionnaire survey a procedure for collecting information by administering questionnaires (documents with questions and space for recording answers) to people who fill them out

Radiant City a community composed of skyscrapers within a park

reconstituted family a family consisting of a man and a woman at least one of whom has been previously married and has a child or children from that prior marriage

reference group a group that provides a basis for evaluating behavior

reinforcers all of the tangible and intangible "things" and events that persons will engage in behaviors to acquire (positive reinforcers) or to escape and avoid (negative reinforcers)

relative deprivation a feeling of unjustified loss or frustration relative to others

relative evaluators people who tend to compare their performance with that of others

reliability of measurement the measurement's lack of variation over time (stability) and consistency when used at the same time in different situations (equivalence)

religion an institution which coordinates theology or beliefs, faith or emotional expression, and ritual or actions, as solutions to problems of ultimate significance in society

replacement rate a completed fertility rate (cfr) equal to 2

repression removal from awareness

research triangulation the use of multiple theories or methods of investigation

resocialization the development of a personality structure that sharply contrasts with the previous personality

resource nonmaterial as well as material factors used to achieve goals

revolution a social movement involving some degree of fundamental social change

revolution of rising expectations a rapid and continuing rise in people's aspirations or goals

riot aggressive and destructive crowd behavior

ritual the formal acting out of a ceremony repeated on certain occasions

role a system of norms and values that provides the script (rules for behavior) for a member of a given social category

role accumulation an expansion of an individual's set of roles or of any role to include elements from others

role conflict contradictory scripts applying to a given individual

role distance degree of resistance against, or disaffection for, a role

role making behavior that rewrites a role's script

role strain personal distress as a result of too many role expectations

role taking behavior in conformity to a role's script

rumor information of unknown origin that is communicated through informal structures

sacred entities phenomena superior in dignity and power to profane things—profoundly differentiated from and often opposed to the latter

sacred society a society legitimating traditionalism and isolation

sacrilization a movement toward a sacred society

sampling procedures techniques for selecting the "sample," or the units to be observed, usually individuals, from the larger population being investigated

satellite cities small manufacturing cities within a metropolitan area, tending to be older than tthe residential suburbs

scale a measurement with numerical properties

scaling procedures techniques designed to achieve precise measurement

scapegoat a person taking the blame for others

scarcity limitations on resources for achieving goals or fulfilling values

science an institution focusing on the continuing development of knowledge based on methods which accept no assumption as sacred

scientific method a process for developing knowledge based on (1) defining a problem, (2) constructing hypotheses or ideas about how to solve the problem, (3) testing these hypotheses, and (4) analyzing the results and drawing conclusions

second law of thermodynamics the principle that all processes within closed and bounded systems move toward disorganization and a state of complete disorder

secondary deviation deviance partially caused by the individual's self-image as a deviant

secondary group a group with few emotional ties

sect a group joined together in protest against existing religious organizations

sector theory ideas linking modes of public transportation to urban patterns best described as "spokes" radiating from the "hub" of the city and dividing it into areas of differential land use

secularization a movement toward a secular society

secular society a society legitimating change, openness to communication, and science

self-evaluators people who tend to assess themselves by comparison to their own previous performances

self-fulfilling prophecy a false definition of the situation evoking a new behavior which makes the originally false conception come true

self-image the individual's view of self

service organization an organization producing intangible products

sex role a social role associated with a given gender

sex-role pluralism a pattern of sex-role relations where each sex role retains its fundamental values and norms yet incorporates elements from the other

sexism prejudice or discrimination against members of a given gender

single-parent family one parent and her or his children

social categories classifications which group individuals together on the basis of certain criteria

social change alteration of social structure in a given direction

social class (1) (Based on Weber) a social category with its members in the same economic situation (2) (Based on Marx) a social category whose members have a similar relationship to the means of production and who, at some point, develop class consciousness

social Darwinism a theory of societal evolution which holds that social change represents inevitable progress toward improved human adaptation to the physical and social environment along a single path

social equality people's similarity in the attainment or possession of whatever society values

social inequality people's differences in the attainment or possession of whatever society values

social interaction action that mutually affects two or more individuals

social mobility the movement of individuals from lower to higher (upward mobility) or higher to lower (downward mobility) social categories in a social stratification system

social movement a collectivity acting with some continuity to promote or resist a change in the society or group of which it is a part

social organization the system of social relationships within a society or group

social relationship a continuing pattern of social interaction

social status (1) degree of honor or prestige given by or received from society (2) position or level on any given plane of stratification

social stratification system a hierarchy (from high to low) of social categories which structures social inequality

social structure (1) a system of shared beliefs, interests, and social relationships (preliminary definition) (2) a system of norms, values, and social relationships

socialization the process by which the individual develops a personality structure and culture is transmitted from one generation to the next

societal evolution a process of change which enhances the adaptive capacity of society

society a group occupying a territory who share the same culture

sociological consciousness awareness of the forces at work in society

sociological imagination the ability to imagine alternatives to existing societal patterns of behavior

sociological practice the application of sociological knowledge to human problems

sociology the science of society

sociology of knowledge the study of the relationship between the knowledge people collect and the social structures surrounding these efforts

sponsored mobility a pattern of educational mobility in which the individual is given elite status by the established elite on the basis of some criterion of supposed merit, usually applied at an early age

Standard Metropolitan Statistical Area (SMSA) an area which includes one or more cities, along with suburbs, having a population of 50,000 or more

state an organization with a monopoly on the legitimate use of force or violence within a society

statistical tests of hypotheses procedures for determining the likelihood that a hypothesis holding true for a sample also holds true for the population from which the sample is drawn

status see **social status**

status inconsistency differences between the individual's positions on several planes of stratification

stereotypes conventional or oversimplified beliefs

strata social categories within a stratification system

structural-functionalism a theoretical orientation emphasizing the functions or contributions made to society by existing social structures

structured exchange a social relationship involving a pattern of positive and negative reinforcers that are sent back and forth

subculture a system of expectations and goals vwidely shared within a subgroup of society

substantive rationality reasoning that involves decisions that are based on a variety of ultimate ends

symbol any phenomenon—such as an object, design, or sound—that represents something other than itself

symbolic interaction interaction based on symbols

symbolic interactionism a theoretical orientation focusing on the individual's definition of the situation, roles, and self-image

system a set of elements related to one another in distinct ways

technology the body of available methods for shaping the physical environment

theology a system of ideas about the nature of society and the universe, and about what should be the human being's relation to them

theory a system of tentative ideas, concepts, or statements about how to solve a problem or about the nature of reality

total institution a place of residence and work where a large number of like-situated individuals, cut off from the wider society for an appreciable period of time, together lead an enclosed, formally administered way of life

traditional authority rule based on conformity to established modes of behavior

traditional education a system of education emphasizing the transmission of knowledge and skills from the past, moral training that conforms to past norms and values, and schools with definite rules that are separated from other organizations

trial marriage a social relationship in which a couple live together without a legal ceremony or a long-range mutual commitment in order to help them decide whether to make their arrangement permanent

trained incapacity the learning of skills which obstruct their manifest purposes

two-career family a family in which the work requirements of the spouses are given equal consideration in all major decisions

unanticipated consequences of purposive action results of goal-directed actions that differ from original expectations

unilinear evolution societal evolution along only one line or path

urban ecologists those who study the human ecology of life in the city

urbanization a rise in the proportion of the

total population of a society that is concentrated within relatively small territorial areas

using available data employing previously recorded information

utilitarian organization an organization people join in order to gain important personal benefits

utopia a positive image of the future

validity of measurement correspondence between the measurement and the variable it is designed to measure

value a goal widely shared within society (or a subgroup of society)

value conflict the conflict inherent in values with opposing goals

variable a characteristic that can vary from one situation to another

vertebrate an organism with a backbone

vertical pattern of a community a community's organized relations to social structures outside of its boundaries

voluntary organization an organization people join because they share the organization's goals

wealth whatever is valued in society, whether nonmaterial or material things